Harvard Business Review

on

ALIGNING TECHNOLOGY WITH STRATEGY

The Harvard Business Review
paperback series

If you need the best practices and ideas for the business challenges you face—but don't have time to find them—*Harvard Business Review* **paperbacks** are for you. Each book is a collection of HBR's inspiring and useful perspectives on a given management topic, all in one place.

The titles include:

Harvard Business Review on Advancing Your Career

Harvard Business Review on Aligning Technology with Strategy

Harvard Business Review on Building Better Teams

Harvard Business Review on Collaborating Effectively

Harvard Business Review on Communicating Effectively

Harvard Business Review on Finding & Keeping the Best People

Harvard Business Review on Fixing Health Care from Inside & Out

Harvard Business Review on Greening Your Business Profitably

Harvard Business Review on Increasing Customer Loyalty

Harvard Business Review on Inspiring & Executing Innovation

Harvard Business Review on Making Smart Decisions

Harvard Business Review on Managing Supply Chains

Harvard Business Review on Rebuilding Your Business Model

Harvard Business Review on Reinventing Your Marketing

Harvard Business Review on Succeeding As an Entrepreneur

Harvard Business Review on Thriving in Emerging Markets

Harvard Business Review on Winning Negotiations

Harvard Business Review

on

ALIGNING TECHNOLOGY WITH STRATEGY

Harvard Business Review Press

Boston, Massachusetts

No part of this publication may be reproduced, stored in or introduced into a retrieval system, or transmitted, in any form, or by any means (electronic, mechanical, photocopying, recording, or otherwise), without the prior permission of the publisher. Requests for permission should be directed to permissions@hbsp.harvard.edu, or mailed to Permissions, Harvard Business School Publishing, 60 Harvard Way, Boston, Massachusetts 02163.

Library of Congress Cataloging-in-Publication Data
Harvard business review on aligning technology with strategy.
     p. cm.—(Harvard business review paperback)
   ISBN 978-1-4221-6247-7 (pbk.) 1. Information technology—
Management. 2. Strategic planning. I. Harvard business review.
   HD30.2.H3748 2011
   658.5'14—dc22
                                                        2010054383

Contents

Harvard
Business
Review

on

ALIGNING
TECHNOLOGY
WITH
STRATEGY

Six IT Decisions Your IT People Shouldn't Make

by Jeanne W. Ross and Peter Weill

FOR SEVERAL YEARS NOW, we have observed the frustration—sometimes even exasperation—that many business executives feel toward information technology and their IT departments. Our center runs a seminar called "IT for the Non-IT Executive," and the refrain among the more than 1,000 senior managers who have taken the course runs something like this: "What can I do? I don't understand IT well enough to manage it in detail. And my IT people—although they work hard—don't seem to understand the very real business problems I face."

Perhaps the complaint we hear most frequently from the executives—most of them CEOs, COOs, CFOs, or other high-ranking officers—is that they haven't realized much business value from the high-priced technology they have installed. Meanwhile, the list of seemingly necessary IT capabilities continues to grow, and IT spending continues to consume an increasing percentage of their budgets. Where's the payback?

Indeed, our research into IT management practices at hundreds of companies around the world has shown that most organizations are not generating the value from IT investments that they could be. The companies that manage their IT investments most successfully generate returns that are as much as 40% higher than those of their competitors.

While a number of factors distinguish these top-performing companies, the most important is that senior managers take a leadership role in a handful of key IT decisions. By contrast, when senior managers abdicate responsibility for those decisions to IT executives, disaster often ensues: Recall the high-profile instances of botched adoptions of large-scale customer-relationship-management and enterprise-resource-planning systems. It would be reasonable to assume that the CRM and ERP fiascoes were the result of technological snafus in getting the complex systems up and running. But in fact the problems generally occurred because senior executives failed to realize that adopting the systems posed a business—not just a technological—challenge. Consequently, they didn't take responsibility for the organizational and business process changes the systems required.

Such unfortunate scenarios are likely to be replayed as companies face the next rounds of IT innovations: the increased use of Web services, the adoption of handheld devices by employees and customers, and the integration of multiple electronic sales and service

Idea in Brief

Gnashing your teeth because your firm's hefty IT investments generate weak returns? Most companies are in the same boat. Worse, some suffer disastrous *losses* owing to mismanaged IT decisions. (Witness companies that sank millions into CRM software—then discovered they didn't need it.)

Why these fiascoes? Many non-IT executives leave key information-technology decisions to IT executives because they don't feel comfortable enough with technology to manage it in detail. Result? IT executives make choices that inadvertently clash with corporate strategy.

IT executives *should* choose information-technology standards, design operations centers, etc. But *non*-IT executives must ensure that IT choices align with company strategy—by making six crucial strategy and execution decisions.

channels such as Web sites, call centers, ATMs, and wireless phones.

Don't get us wrong. IT executives are the right people to make numerous decisions about IT management—the choice of technology standards, the design of the IT operations center, the technical expertise the organization will need, the standard methodology for implementing new systems. But an IT department should not be left to make, often by default, the choices that determine the impact of IT on a company's business strategy.

To help senior managers avoid IT disasters—and, more important, to help them generate real value from their IT investments—we offer a list of six decisions for which they would be wise to take leadership responsibility. The first three have to do with strategy; the second three relate to execution. Each is a decision that IT people shouldn't be making—because, in the end, that's not their job.

Idea in Practice

Strategy Decisions

1. **How much should we spend on IT?** Define crystal-clear IT goals. A vague vision (e.g., "providing information to anyone, anytime, anywhere") can mean millions wasted on chasing elusive benefits. *Then* set IT funding to achieve those goals.

2. **Which business processes should receive our IT dollars?** Decide which IT initiatives will further your strategy—and fund only those. You'll avoid burying your IT department in irrelevant projects.

   Example: Delta Air Lines overhauled its IT investment approach when its business units' disparate IT systems began hindering employees' ability to serve customers. A single question ("At what gate will my plane arrive?")

could generate 17 different answers. Delta's response? A new, *unified* technology platform providing all employees with current flight and customer information. Simultaneously, Delta shelved a revenue-planning system—competition for additional IT resources would have threatened the new platform's success.

3. **Which IT capabilities should be firmwide?** Centralizing IT capabilities can save money—but limit business units' flexibility. Yet *excess* flexibility is expensive and can dilute units' synergies. Weigh these tradeoffs.

   Example: After a century of operating as 200 decentralized units worldwide, Johnson & Johnson had to rethink its response to a new breed of customer with scant patience for

---

1. How much should we spend on IT?

Given the uncertain returns on IT spending, many executives wonder whether they are spending too much—or perhaps even too little. If we can just get the dollar amount right, the thinking goes, the other IT issues will take care of themselves. So they look to industry

multiple salespersons, invoices, and shipments. It introduced a centralized global desktop that provided "a single view of the customer" (e.g., standardized account numbers) and enabled cross-unit electronic communication—but maintained individualization at regional levels.

Execution Decisions

4. **How good do our IT services need to be?** Obviously, an IT system that doesn't work is useless. But don't let IT executives push for "Cadillac" service when a "Buick" will do. Determine how much reliability, responsiveness, and data accessibility you *must* have—and don't waste money on the rest. For Dow Corning, a brief downtime—though inconvenient—wouldn't halt production. So the company built a back-up site for use only if its system crashed for several hours.

5. **What security and privacy risks will we accept?** Weigh tradeoffs between privacy versus convenience. When Yale University let applicants access their admissions decision online, Princeton officials—competing for those students—accessed the site, too.

6. **Whom do we blame if an IT initiative fails?** The IT department is responsible for delivering systems on time and within budget. *Your* job? To make organizational changes that generate business value from those systems. Designate "sponsors" to assign resources to IT initiatives, establish success metrics, and oversee implementation.

benchmarks as a way of determining appropriate spending levels.

But in the successful companies we have studied, senior managers approach the question very differently. First they determine the strategic role that IT will play in the organization, and only then do they establish a companywide funding level that will enable technology to fulfill that objective.

IT goals vary considerably across organizations. They may be relatively modest: for example, eliminating inaccuracies and inefficiencies in administrative processes. Or they may be central to a company's strategy: for example, supporting a seamless global supply chain, flawless customer service, or leading-edge research and development. Clearly, these different objectives require different levels of spending. And if you have determined that technology should play a central strategic role, the nature of that role will affect the required level of spending.

Take arch rivals United Parcel Service and FedEx. Both companies report spending around $1 billion on IT each year, but FedEx, which has annual revenues of about $20 billion, is just two-thirds the size of UPS. Does that mean IT plays a more important role at FedEx? No, simply a different one. UPS's IT strategy, which evolved from its industrial engineering roots, has focused on introducing efficiencies to a business that demands consistency and reliability. The company's centralized, standardized IT environment allows for dependable customer service at a relatively low cost. FedEx, on the other hand, has focused on achieving flexibility to meet the needs of its various customer segments. The higher costs of this decentralized approach to IT management are offset by the benefits of localized innovation and a heightened ability to respond to customers' needs.

Of course, UPS also uses technology to meet the needs of individual customers, and FedEx uses technology to provide consistent service across customer segments. But the thrusts of the two companies' IT and business strategies are different. Both are successful because they have matched their spending levels to those strategies—not to industry benchmarks.

In most companies, senior management has not defined IT's role so clearly, in effect abdicating that responsibility to IT people. In those organizations, the IT department can deliver on individual projects but can't build a "strategic platform," one that not only responds to immediate needs but also provides escalating benefits over the long term.

UPS's experience illustrates the benefits of a broad strategic platform. The company began investing heavily in IT in the late 1980s, at a time when FedEx was touting its package-tracking capability. But instead of simply creating a tracking system, UPS's senior management decided to build a comprehensive package database that had the potential to become a platform for numerous applications. To gather information for the database, UPS developed the Delivery Information Acquisition Device, a handheld computer used by drivers to collect customers' signatures and other information electronically. The device saved drivers 30 minutes a day by reducing the manual input of delivery information. But these electronic tracking capabilities were only an initial benefit. The electronic data provided a more accurate record of deliveries, enabling UPS to collect hundreds of millions of dollars in revenues that had been lost when customers self-reported deliveries, which UPS couldn't easily verify. In subsequent years,

What Happens When Senior Managers Ignore Their IT Responsibilities?

	IT Decision	Senior Management's Role	Consequences of Abdicating the Decision
Strategy	How much should we spend on IT?	Define the strategic role that IT will play in the company and then determine the level of funding needed to achieve that objective.	The company fails to develop an IT platform that furthers its strategy, despite high IT spending.
	Which business processes should receive our IT dollars?	Make clear decisions about which IT initiatives will and will not be funded.	A lack of focus overwhelms the IT unit, which tries to deliver many projects that may have little companywide value or can't be implemented well simultaneously.
	Which IT capabilities need to be company-wide?	Decide which IT capabilities should be provided centrally and which should be developed by individual businesses.	Excessive technical and process standardization limits the flexibility of business units, or frequent exceptions to the standards increase costs and limit business synergies.
Execution	How good do our IT services really need to be?	Decide which features – for example, enhanced reliability or response time – are needed on the basis of their costs and benefits.	The company may pay for service options that, given its priorities, aren't worth the costs.
	What security and privacy risks will we accept?	Lead the decision making on the trade-off between security and privacy on one hand and convenience on the other.	An overemphasis on security and privacy may inconvenience customers, employees, and suppliers; an underemphasis may make data vulnerable.
	Whom do we blame if an IT initiative fails?	Assign a business executive to be accountable for every IT project; monitor business metrics.	The business value of the system is never realized.

the database allowed UPS to introduce new products, such as guaranteed delivery, and new processes, including on-line package tracking by customers. Recent enhancements will optimize the scheduling of routes and help UPS's business customers get paid faster once their goods are delivered.

Those benefits grew out of UPS's decision to make significant and consistent investments in a system that, before long, outgrew its original purpose. UPS's CEO, Mike Eskew, calls the new applications, each of which furthers the strategy of providing consistent and reliable customer service, "happy surprises." Such unforeseen benefits lead to a total return on IT investment that exceeds the sum of the ROIs of individual projects—a return far greater than many companies can imagine.

IT spending can be designed to meet immediate needs and allow for an array of future benefits only if IT and business goals are clearly defined. Some management teams offer only a vague vision—for example, "providing information to anyone, anytime, anywhere." IT units respond to such ill-defined goals by trying to build platforms capable of responding to any business need. Not surprisingly, the typical outcome of such large, undirected projects is millions of dollars spent chasing elusive benefits.

2. Which business processes should receive our IT dollars?

As most executives know, IT initiatives can multiply quickly. We have seen companies of a few hundred

Why Not Just Outsource IT?

GIVEN THE POTENTIAL HEADACHES OF managing IT, it is tempting to hand the job over to someone else. Indeed, outsourcing once appeared to be a simple solution to management frustrations, and senior management teams at many companies negotiated contracts with large service providers to run their entire IT functions. At a minimum, these providers were often able to provide IT capabilities for a lower cost and with fewer hassles than the companies had been able to themselves.

But many of these outsourcing arrangements resulted in dissatisfaction, particularly as a company's business needs changed. Service providers, with their standard offerings and detailed contracts, provided IT capabilities that weren't flexible enough to meet changing requirements, and they often seemed slow to respond to problems. Furthermore, a relationship with a supplier often required substantial investments of money and time, which entrenched that supplier in the company's strategic planning and business processes. The company then became particularly vulnerable if the supplier failed to meet its contractual obligations.

Not surprisingly, other problems arose because senior managers, in choosing to outsource the IT function, were also outsourcing

people that have a few hundred IT projects under way. Clearly, not all of them are equally important. But we find that senior managers are often reluctant to step in and choose between the projects that will have a significant impact on the company's success and those that provide some benefits but aren't essential.

Leaving such decisions in the hands of the IT department means that IT executives set the priorities for what are in fact important business issues—or, just as troubling, they try to deliver on every project a business responsibility for one or more of the crucial decisions they should have been making themselves. Indeed, companies often hired outside providers because they were dissatisfied with the performance of their own IT departments—but that dissatisfaction was primarily the result of their own lack of involvement.

In light of this track record, most bigger companies, at least, are deciding to keep their main IT capabilities in-house. But many engage in selective outsourcing. Good candidates for this are commodity services—such as telecommunications, in which there are several competing suppliers and specifications are easy to set—and services involving technologies with which the company lacks expertise.

Unlike decisions to outsource the entire IT function, selective outsourcing decisions are usually best left to the IT unit—assuming that senior management has taken responsibility for the six key decisions. For example, once the acceptable level of security and privacy risk is determined, IT executives can research competitive offerings and conduct the cost-benefit analysis for completing these projects internally versus externally.

manager claims is important. Presented with a list of approved and funded projects, most IT units will do their best to carry them out. But this typically leads to a backlog of delayed initiatives and an overwhelmed and demoralized IT department.

The failure of senior managers to choose a manageable set of IT priorities can also lead to disaster. One need only remember Hershey Foods' infamous decision in 1999 to implement several major systems simultaneously, including CRM, ERP, and supply chain management, which ultimately resulted in the company's inability to deliver candy to important customers during the Halloween season.

Contrast this with Delta Air Lines' disciplined approach to IT investment in recent years. In 1997, the company was facing a technology crisis. Several years before, the airline had outsourced its corporate IT function, which prompted individual business units, unhappy with the service they were receiving, to create their own IT capabilities. (For a discussion of outsourcing, see the sidebar "Why Not Just Outsource IT?") Running disparate systems across the units made it difficult for employees to provide timely, accurate customer service. One question—for example, "At what gate will my plane arrive?"—could conceivably generate 17 different answers, depending on which system an employee checked. In addition, many of the systems were based on older technologies that might not perform properly with the arrival of the year 2000.

In a move as farsighted as UPS's decision to create a package database, Delta's senior managers opted to use the Y2K threat to build a powerful technology platform, dubbed the Delta Nervous System (DNS), to provide real-time information for flight operations and customer service. The three-year, $1 billion project would provide every employee with constant updates on the status of any flight or customer. As the managers defined the vision for this system, they made another critical decision: They would not invest simultaneously in a new revenue-planning system. Such systems help airlines make complex decisions concerning scheduling, pricing, equipment configuration, and routing that directly affect profitability. But Delta knew it couldn't address all of its technology needs at once. Given the limitations of the company's IT and business resources, additional projects would have threatened the success of the DNS. So the company put a new revenue-planning system, also key to Delta's strategy, on hold until 2002, when the DNS was in place.

3. Which IT capabilities need to be companywide?

Increasingly, executives are recognizing the significant cost savings and strategic benefits that come from centralizing IT capabilities and standardizing IT infrastructure across an organization. This approach leverages technology expertise across the company, permits large and cost-effective contracts with software suppliers, and facilitates global business processes. At the same time, though, standards can restrict the flexibility of individual business units, limit the company's responsiveness to differentiated customer segments, and generate strong resistance from business unit managers.

When IT executives are left to make decisions about what will and will not be centralized and standardized, they typically take one of two approaches. Depending on the company's culture, either they insist on standardizing everything to keep costs low or, recognizing the importance of business unit autonomy, they grant exceptions to corporate standards to any business unit manager who raises a stink. The former approach restricts the flexibility of business units; the latter is expensive and limits business synergies. In some instances, systems using different standards can actually work against one another, resulting in a corporate IT infrastructure whose total value may be *less* than the sum of its parts. Consequently, senior managers should play the lead role in weighing these crucial trade-offs.

The experience of Johnson & Johnson, the global consumer and health care company, illustrates the challenges of achieving the right balance when trying to impose companywide standards. For almost 100 years, J&J enjoyed success as a decentralized organization. By the early 1990s, though, it had encountered a powerful new breed of customer with no patience for the multiple salespersons, invoices, and shipments that resulted from doing business with more than one of the company's roughly 200 operating units. J&J's management had to decide how to reconcile the growing need to act as a unified company with its historical preference for business unit autonomy. IT would be central to the resolution.

A key IT decision involved data standards. Senior managers quickly realized that global data definitions, which would facilitate information sharing among business units, would be difficult to implement. Over the years, data items such as product codes, product costs, and customer accounts had been defined locally to meet the needs of operating units in different countries. Accordingly, the company's senior managers formed a team to define the limited set of standard data definitions needed to provide a single view of the customer. The remainder could be determined at the regional or business unit level. Achieving a single view of the customer also required a single technology base, one that allowed electronic communication across units. So J&J broke with tradition and instituted corporate, rather than business unit, funding for the implementation of a standardized workstation with a standardized interface to J&J corporate systems and data. Over time, J&J has continued to shift IT capabilities from the business units to centralized systems. It has moved cautiously, though, recognizing that a sudden shift to a more standardized environment could be disruptive.

Management teams in every company, whether centralized or decentralized, must constantly assess the balance between companywide and business-unit IT capabilities. Traditionally centralized organizations like UPS find that their shared infrastructures sometimes do not meet the needs of new, smaller businesses. Thus, they have gradually introduced some localized capabilities in the same way that the traditionally diversified J&J has introduced centralized ones.

4. How good do our IT services really need to be?

An IT system that doesn't work is useless. But that doesn't mean every system must be wrapped in gold-plated functionality. Characteristics such as reliability, responsiveness, and data accessibility come at a cost. It is up to senior managers to decide how much they are willing to spend for various features and services.

For some companies, top-of-the-line service is not negotiable. Investment banks do not debate how much data they can afford to lose if a trading system crashes; 100% recovery is a requirement. Similarly, Gtech Corporation, the company that runs the majority of the world's government-sponsored lotteries, cannot compromise on response time. Most of its contracts in the United States specify that customers will receive their lottery tickets within five seconds—and it takes three seconds just to print the ticket. Nor can Gtech afford any downtime: State governments specify penalties as high as $10,000 per minute if the system is unavailable. This is a fairly compelling justification for ensuring that computers will continue to run despite floods, tornadoes, power outages, and telecommunications breakdowns, regardless of the cost.

But not every company is a Gtech or a Merrill Lynch. Most can tolerate limited downtime or occasionally slow response times, and they must weigh the problems these create against the cost of preventing them. Consider Dow Corning. The nature of the company's operations means that a brief downtime of its ERP system would be an inconvenience but would not stop production or result in lost customer orders. Although senior managers wanted to prevent all downtime, the cost was prohibitive. So in 1999, when they decided to build a backup, or "hot," site, they opted for one that would be used only if the system went down for several hours. The company periodically reviews its backup capability and in the past few years has been able to reduce its risk even more as technologies become more affordable.

Decisions concerning the appropriate levels of IT service need to be made by senior business managers. Left to their own devices, IT units are likely to opt for the highest levels—providing Cadillac service when a Buick will do—because the IT unit will be judged on such things as how often the system goes down. Typically, the cost of higher levels of service is built into the price of IT systems and is neither broken out nor discussed separately. IT people should provide a menu of service options and prices to help managers understand what they are paying for. Business managers should then, in consultation with IT managers, determine the appropriate level of service at a price they can afford.

This kind of analysis can have an impact not only on onetime IT investments but also on annual operating costs, a contentious issue at many companies. In many cases, fixed costs can be significantly reduced if managers establish, during system development, lower expectations for requirements such as reliability and response time. Conversely, the analysis might reveal that the company is underestimating its risk of downtime and has not sufficiently protected itself against it.

5. What security and privacy risks will we accept?

Security, like reliability and responsiveness, is a feature of IT systems that requires companies to weigh the level of protection they want against the amount they are willing to spend. In this case, though, there is another trade-off: Increasing security involves not only higher costs but also greater inconvenience.

Take our own organization, MIT. Because the institute is a particularly attractive target for hackers keen to show off their skills, MIT has developed a state-of-the-art security system that successfully repels a continuous stream of attacks. It features a firewall different from the type most organizations use to limit external access to their internal systems. But although it provides greater protection, MIT's nonstandard approach means that the institute cannot install most commercial software packages for applications such as course registration and student accounting. MIT sees these limitations as a cost of doing business, but many private companies would likely find such extraordinary security efforts to be too costly and onerous.

As global privacy protections increasingly become mandated by government, security takes on new importance: Well-designed privacy protections can be compromised by inadequate system security. Yale University's decision to allow applicants access to their admissions decision by providing their dates of birth and Social Security numbers, while convenient for users, allowed an official at Princeton University, which was competing for the same students, to access the site with ease. Financial services firms face similar threats when they design systems that give customers quick and easy electronic access to their accounts. Telephone companies that allow on-line payment of bills render vulnerable the records of customers' telephone calls. In every case, these organizations are—consciously or not—making the trade-offs between customers' convenience and privacy.

It is up to senior managers to assess those trade-offs. Many IT units will adopt a philosophy that absolute security is its responsibility and will simply deny access anytime it cannot be provided safely. But try running that idea by a bank's marketing executives, who are counting on simplified on-line transactions to attract new customers.

6. Whom do we blame if an IT initiative fails?

The recurring concern we hear from executives in our courses—that IT efforts fail to generate the intended business benefits—is often accompanied by some finger-pointing: There must be something wrong with the IT function in our company. We have found, however, that the problem more often reveals that something is wrong with the way non-IT executives are managing IT-enabled change in the organization.

Look at those well-publicized examples of ERP and CRM initiatives that never generated measurable value. Invariably, the failures resulted from assumptions that IT units or consultants could implement the systems while business managers went about their daily tasks. In fact, new systems alone have no value; value derives from new or redesigned business processes. We recall the experience of a midsize manufacturing company that had installed an expensive ERP system with no apparent impact. A new CEO came on board and, impressed by the system's potential and the fact that no one was using it, reorganized the company's business processes to take advantage of its capabilities. He attributed the company's ability to turn a profit for the first time in five years to this reorganization. Think of the benefits that might have been realized if the system had been designed to serve specific processes in the first place.

To avoid disasters, senior managers need to assign business executives to take responsibility for realizing the business benefits of an IT initiative. These "sponsors" need authority to assign resources to projects and time to oversee the creation and implementation of those projects. They should meet regularly with IT personnel, arrange training for users, and work with the IT department to establish clear metrics for determining the initiative's success. Such sponsors can ensure that new IT systems deliver real business value; blaming the IT department reflects a misunderstanding about what that group can deliver.

IT success may also require a sustained commitment on the part of the managers who will use and benefit from the technology. Take the case of the Longitudinal Medical Record system, introduced in 1998 at Partners HealthCare, a Boston-based umbrella organization of major hospitals and local clinics. From the beginning, the managers—in this case, a cadre of practicing physicians in management roles—took full responsibility for extracting value from the LMR's new technology. For every patient they see, the physicians are supposed to enter electronically, in a standard format, all diagnosis and treatment information so that the system can highlight key facts for physicians examining the patient in the future. Deploying the LMR posed significant technological challenges, but the greater challenges were organizational: The system required physicians to spend precious time on data entry using a tool that was far from perfect in its early versions.

The physicians participating in the initiative have continued to play a role in the development of this IT system, a role that goes far beyond helping to define requirements. They must use the system (even though the technology sometimes breaks down), provide constant feedback on its features (so the IT unit can make continual improvements), and encourage colleagues to sign on to the project (because its value is limited until its use becomes widespread).

Unless managers take responsibility for the success— and failure—of IT systems, they will end up with systems that, while perhaps technically elegant, will have no impact on the business. The IT department should be held responsible for delivering systems that are on time and on budget and that have the potential to be both useful and used. But only business executives can be held responsible for making the organizational changes needed to generate business value from a new system. Until they accept this responsibility, companies cannot hope to eliminate complaints about having spent too much money for too little value.

While we firmly believe that senior business executives err when they abdicate responsibility for these six IT decisions, we aren't advocating that any of the decisions be made unilaterally in the executive suite.

Clearly, such complex issues can't be dealt with in a single senior management meeting at which executives lay down mandates for IT spending, management, and use. Although senior managers need to ensure that IT spending and initiatives are aligned with and further the company's strategy and goals, such decisions are best made with input from both business unit and IT executives.

Instead of approaching IT decision making in an ad hoc manner, companies increasingly are establishing formal IT governance structures that specify how IT decisions are made, carried out, reinforced, and even challenged. Such structures apply principles similar to those of financial governance—for example, who is authorized to commit the company to a contract or how cash flow is managed across the enterprise.

A company can choose from a variety of fundamentally different governance approaches depending on its culture, strategy, and structure. But good IT governance identifies who should be responsible and accountable for critical IT decisions. For example, decisions about IT investment are often made as part of the companywide budgeting process approved by senior management. Decisions about IT architectures and the associated standards are often made by committees with both technical and business membership. In all cases, though, effective governance ensures that IT-related decisions embody uniform principles about the role IT plays in the organization.

IT has long been a key to the success of State Street Corporation, a leading global financial-services firm. But although nearly one-quarter of its operating expense budget typically has been devoted to technology, until recently there was no companywide IT budget, and almost all spending decisions were made by the individual business units. To ensure that IT decisions supported the company's new strategy of presenting a single face to customers across business units, State Street recently established an Information Technology Executive Committee. The committee, whose members include the COO, the CIO, and the heads of the business units, meets every two months. It is responsible for setting IT direction within the context of State Street's strategy and then balancing companywide and business unit needs to create a single IT budget for the company.

Under State Street's IT governance structure, the CIO plays an active role in setting the company's IT strategy and facilitating the effective use of IT. At the same time, however, note the level of commitment shown by the company's business leaders, including the COO. In that sense, State Street is an illustration of the proposition that there are key IT decisions your IT people shouldn't make—on their own.

JEANNE W. ROSS is a principal research scientist and **PETER WEILL** is a senior research scientist and the chair of the Center for Information Systems Research at the MIT Sloan School of Management.

Originally published in November 2002. Reprint R0211F

Getting IT Right

by Charlie S. Feld and Donna B. Stoddard

OF ALL THE MEMBERS OF the executive committee, the CIO is the least understood—mostly because his profession is still so young. Over the centuries, the fields of manufacturing, finance, sales, marketing, and engineering have evolved into a set of commonly understood practices, with established vocabularies and operating principles comprehended by every member of the senior team. By contrast, the field of information technology—born only 40 years ago with the advent of the IBM 360 in 1964—is prepubescent.

This generation gap means that, in most organizations, the corporate parent—caught in the linguistic chasm between tech-speak and business-speak—has no idea what its youngest child is up to. Management too often shrugs its shoulders, hands the kid a fat allowance, and looks the other way. Later on, the company finds it's paid an outrageous price for the latest technological fad. Instead of addressing the problem, many companies just kick the kid out of the house.

The result in many major corporations is that IT is an expensive mess. Orders are lost. Customers call help desks that aren't helpful. Tracking systems don't track. Indeed, the average business fritters away 20% of its corporate IT budget on purchases that fail to achieve their objectives, according to Gartner Research. This adds up to approximately $500 billion wasted worldwide.

Such waste—most egregious in industries like transportation, insurance, telecommunications, banking, and manufacturing—is a direct result of the fact that IT has so far operated without the constructive involvement of the senior management team, despite the best intentions of CIOs. Over the years, IT departments have enthusiastically fulfilled requests by different corporate functions. In the process, companies have created and populated dozens of legacy information systems, each consisting of millions of lines of code, that do not talk to one another. As the data from discrete functions collect in separate databases, more and more resources are required merely to keep the systems functioning properly.

While the Y2K crisis impelled many companies to clean up the worst of their legacy systems, most organizations merely did spring cleaning, ignoring the fact that their technological houses badly needed structural repair. Despite advances in technology, most companies continue to struggle with 35-year-old, costly, and rigid information archeology; a cynical executive board; a discouraged IT organization; and throngs of increasingly frustrated customers. Add the confusion of mergers and acquisitions and a long march of poorly implemented "solutions" (ERP, CRM, data warehouses,

Idea in Brief

Modern information technology started four decades ago, yet in most major corporations IT remains an expensive mess. This is partly because the relatively young and rapidly evolving practice of IT continues to be either grossly misunderstood or blindly ignored by top management. In this article, the authors say a systematic approach to understanding and executing IT can and should be implemented, and it should be organized along three interconnected principles: (1) *A long-term IT renewal plan linked to corporate strategy.* Such a plan focuses the entire IT group on the company's overarching goals during a multiyear period, makes appropriate investments directed toward cutting costs in the near term, and generates a detailed blueprint for long-term systems rejuvenation and value creation. (2) *A simplified, unifying corporate technology platform.* Instead of relying on vertically oriented data silos that serve individual corporate units (HR, accounting, and so on), companies adopt a clean, horizontally oriented architecture designed to serve the whole organization. (3) *A highly functional, performance-oriented IT organization.* Instead of functioning as if it were different from the rest of the firm or as a loose confederation of tribes, the IT department works as a team and operates according to corporate performance standards.

portals, mobile computing, dashboards, and outsourcing), and you end up with chaos. How can this situation possibly be set right?

Making IT work has little to do with technology itself. Just because a builder can acquire a handsome set of hammers, nails, and planks doesn't mean he can erect a quality house at reasonable cost. Making IT work demands the same things that other parts of the business do—inspired leadership, superb execution, motivated people, and the thoughtful attention and high expectations of senior management.

IT success also requires common understanding. Senior managers know how to talk about finances, because they all speak or understand the language and can agree on a common set of metrics (profit and loss, balance sheets, return on assets, and so on). They can do the same with most elements of operations, customer service, and marketing. So why not with IT? There is no longer any reason why nontechnical executives should allow themselves to be befuddled by IT discussions or bedazzled by three-letter acronyms. And there is no reason that technologists cannot learn to speak the language of business and become perfectly good leaders.

We believe that there are three interdependent, interrelated, and universally applicable principles for executing IT effectively and that it is top management's responsibility to understand and help apply them. The three principles are:

A Long-Term IT Renewal Plan Linked to Corporate Strategy. Revamping IT is like renewing a major urban area while people are living there. The effort requires a plan that keeps the entire IT group focused on the company's overarching goals during a multiyear period, makes appropriate investments directed toward near-term cost reduction, and generates a detailed blueprint for long-term systems rejuvenation and value creation.

A Simplified, Unifying Corporate Technology Platform. Such a platform replaces a wide variety of vertically oriented data silos that serve individual corporate units (HR, accounting, and so on) with a clean, horizontally oriented architecture designed to serve the company as a whole. This is similar to selecting standard-sized pipes and connectors for a city plan.

A Highly Functional, Performance-Oriented IT Organization. Instead of being treated as if it were different from the rest of the firm or as a loose confederation of tribes, the IT department works as a team and operates according to corporate performance standards.

Like interlocking gears, these principles work together and must be consistently applied. If they mesh well, each reinforces the others. If one is disengaged or turns in the wrong direction, the whole machine starts working against itself or grinds to a halt.

As a CIO, Charlie Feld has successfully applied these principles to rejuvenate IT at a number of *Fortune* 100 companies—first at Frito-Lay, then during his career as CIO at corporations such as Delta Air Lines and Burlington Northern and Santa Fe Railroads. What follows is a composite of his experiences, which illustrates the three principles in context.

Gear 1: A Long-Term IT Plan

Because the rate of technological change is so rapid, and the job tenure of CIOs generally brief, most people see IT through the narrow lens of short-term, silver-bullet solutions. Heaven knows, vendors want you to believe that their important new technologies will blow away what has come before. You can't blame a salesperson for trying to sell, or CIOs for having a queasy buy-or-lose feeling, but this attitude is precisely the opposite of the one companies should be taking. We would argue that because the winds of change buffet IT more than any other area of the organization, IT benefits most from a long-term, disciplined, strategic view, and a square focus on achieving the company's most fundamental goals.

For example, Frito-Lay's strategic goal has always been to make, move, and sell tasty, fresh snack foods as rapidly and efficiently as possible. That goal hasn't changed since the 1930s, when founder Herman Lay ran his business from his Atlanta kitchen and delivery truck. He bought and cooked the potatoes. He delivered the chips to stores. He collected the money and knew all his customers. He balanced the books and did his own quality assurance. Herman Lay knew how to conduct the perfect "sense and respond" e-business before such a thing ever existed, for he held real-time customer, accounting, and inventory information all in one place— his head.

After years of spectacular growth, the company grew more and more distracted from this simple business model. By the early 1980s, the company's sales force had swelled to 10,000, and information grew harder and harder to manage. The company's old batch-based data processing systems were all driven by paper forms that took 12 weeks to print and distribute to the sales force. All sales transactions were recorded by hand;

reams of disparate data were transferred to the company's mainframe computers. Much was lost in the process of setting up a dozen different functional organizations and a variety of databases, none of which communicated with each other.

This modus operandi made it impossible to change prices quickly or develop new regional promotions, streamline production, or improve inventory management. It was as if Herman Lay's company had suffered a spinal cord injury, with the brain and the body no longer connected. At the same time, the company was seeing the rise of strong regional competitors. The leaders realized that if trends continued as they were, its overall revenues would fall significantly by the early 1990s.

Mike Jordan, who took over as CEO of Frito-Lay in 1983, decided to tackle the problem. He reconstructed the company as a hybrid organization that was neither totally centralized nor decentralized. His goal was to teach the company to "walk and chew gum at the same time," as he put it, by separating out the company's two competitive advantages: the purchasing, production, and distribution leverages of a national powerhouse, and the local resources that gave the company regional speed and agility. All this led to an organizational design that kept purchasing, manufacturing, distribution, systems, accounting, and R&D as the centralized platform, leaving the decentralized sales and marketing organizations to launch their store-by-store and street-by-street offensives.

Having identified the company's strategy, Jordan then developed a long-term IT renewal (as opposed to a "rip and replace") plan. An executive committee—comprised of the CEO, CFO, CIO, and two executive vice presidents—outlined a shift from paper to a risky, emerging handheld technology for the salespeople on the street, as well as a transformation from batch accounting to online operational systems. The goal was to digitally reconnect the company's nervous system. Equipped with the cool new handhelds, the sales force would be able to manage price, inventory, and customer changes in real time and connect to the supply pipeline. The handheld computers would also establish a technological "beachhead"—one sufficiently important to keep the business's attention and achieve fast operating results.

Paying for all this, of course, would not be easy. The journey would take from 1984 to 1988, at a huge cost (at the time): $40 million for the handhelds and about $100 million for the databases and core systems. Some on the executive committee balked, arguing that efficiencies gained by the technology would be lost by salespeople working fewer hours. But the company had no choice but to revitalize its regional sales, and though the systems overhaul would be costly, staying put would be even costlier.

To fund the new computers, Jordan set up a long-term, ongoing funding mechanism designed to keep IT spending both predictable and fairly stable from year to year. To get things rolling, each sales region had to commit to a reduction in selling expenses from 22 cents on the dollar to 21 cents within a year of the handhelds' installation. The savings would be achieved by increasing sales at constant cost, reducing costs, or a combination of the two.

The scheme worked: With the new system in place, the company saved between 30,000 to 50,000 hours of paperwork per week. By 1988, savings resulting from better control over sales data came to more than $40 million per year—savings that in turn funded the renewal of the core data systems. Frito-Lay was able to cut the number of its distribution centers, reduce stale product by 50%, and increase its domestic revenues from $3 billion in 1986 to $4.2 billion by 1989. Today, Frito-Lay continues to be the dominant player in the snack-food industry.

Frito-Lay's technology story received a lot of press at the time, mostly because the handheld technology was sexy. But notice what the story was really about: It was about executing Herman Lay's original, real-time business experience—feeling the money jingling in the pocket and seeing the inventory in the truck.

Gear 2: A Unifying Platform

Most IT organizations are amazingly complex and have individual initiatives that are like independent countries, each with its own business applications, technologies, culture, data definitions, and orientation. Project costs soar because individual teams are isolated rather than harnessed together, and few teams reuse each other's components—a condition exacerbated by a plethora of consultants and competitive technologies. And when a company is running hundreds of heterogeneous hardware and software systems, costs run rampant.

Consider the cost of such complexity at Delta Air Lines. In 1997, Delta's fleet consisted of 600 airplanes and a rainbow of models, ranging from 727s, 737s, 757s, to 767s, from MD 80s and 90s to L1011s. (By contrast, Southwest Airlines operates only one kind of airplane.) Each plane carried different instrumentation from different eras; as a result, the company needed to train pilots and crew members to operate the different models. Keeping track of aircraft, people, parts inventory, qualified mechanics, handling equipment, and catering carts all added to the structural cost of the airline. Delta's new CEO, Leo Mullin, and his executive team understood that if they reduced the number of plane types they operated, they could lower annual costs by hundreds of millions of dollars.

What the executives didn't understand was that they had an even worse problem in their IT organization. The company was running more than 30 major IT platforms, with 60 million lines of code, none of which were integrated with each other. Each platform required approximately 100 IT support specialists to keep the systems up and running. That arrangement cost the company about $700 million per year in capital and operating expenses. The problem within IT made the air fleet look like a model of simplicity. Running the airline was nearly impossible. Gate changes by the tower systems were not received in time by the people who needed them: the crews, caterers, reservation agents, ticket counter agents, mechanics, baggage handlers, and customers. The gate-change data were locked inside individual and often conflicting systems.

Once it understood the root cause of complexity, Delta's executive team agreed to a long-term simplification project. Delta launched an effort to build an IT organization that spoke a common language, operated against a simple and well-understood set of principles, and created an architecture that included a common set of databases. Everyone in the IT organization focused on a consistent set of methods, technologies, and management disciplines.

From 1998 to 2003, Delta refocused its formerly decentralized IT investments of $200 million to $300 million annually on a unified IT architecture called the Delta Nervous System, which cut inefficiencies out of virtually every area of its operation. Like Frito-Lay's system, Delta reconnected the electronic brain (IT) to the physical body (operations) by linking the customer, flight, schedule, and employee databases that keep track of everything from reservations to ticketing to check-in and baggage handling to crew operations.

The foundation of the Delta Nervous System was a comprehensive and aggressive simplification effort within the IT architecture to keep the number of moving parts to a minimum. To rebuild and simplify its IT systems, Delta took a radically different tack. Rebuilding the systems from scratch would have been extremely costly—plus the company had an airline to run. Instead, Delta built a new set of software, or middleware, that connected a common infrastructure with every application. The middleware within the Delta

The silo-based organization versus the layered organization

Delta's IT architecture was once made up of a series of silos. Different parts of the company used different applications and disconnected databases, leading to redundancy, increased costs, and overall organizational dysfunction.

To rebuild and simplify its IT systems, Delta introduced a common layer of middleware that connected the company's electronic brain (IT) to its physical body (operations). Sitting on top of the old transaction systems, the middleware carried key operational data from one application to another: Customer, flight, schedule, and employee databases were connected to reservations, ticketing, check-in, baggage handling, and crew operations. Delta could then upgrade or replace older systems where necessary, without disrupting the underlying IT system.

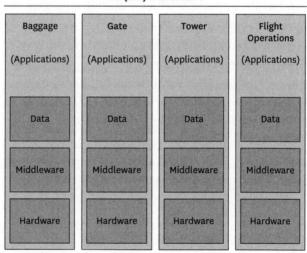

Old (silo) architecture

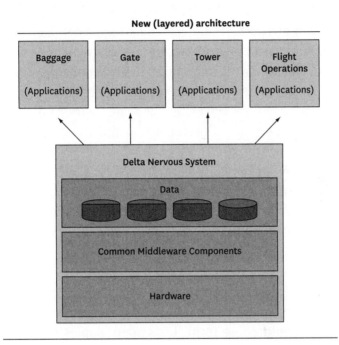

New (layered) architecture

Baggage	Gate	Tower	Flight Operations
(Applications)	(Applications)	(Applications)	(Applications)

Delta Nervous System

Data

Common Middleware Components

Hardware

Nervous System sat on top of the old transaction systems and carried critical operational data from one application to the other. If a gate changed, the middleware pushed the news to the other systems that needed to know about the change (catering, crew, gate agent, baggage tracking, and so on). With this middleware in place, Delta could then go back and upgrade or replace older systems where necessary, without disrupting the IT system as a whole. (For a visual of the Delta Nervous System, see the exhibit "The Silo-Based Organization Versus the Layered Organization.")

The middleware layer within the Delta Nervous System proved essential to leveraging technology innovation at Delta. It allowed the company to add new technology in a simpler and less risky manner over time. Most companies go through the agonizing work of rewriting their systems as technology changes. Delta, however, did the opposite. For example, Delta disconnected the manual systems that fed the operations control center (OCC) and reconnected them to the Delta Nervous System. This effectively rejuvenated the OCC without resorting to radical surgery or replacement. The OCC became a vibrant, fully functioning participant in the Delta Nervous System at a fraction of the cost.

The design of Delta's nervous system also formed the road map and contract between IT teams, providing guidance on how data would be stored, where the data would come from, how many copies the company would keep, as well as rules for calculating and interpreting the data. For example, all systems (operations control center, tower, gate, passenger, and crew) could now agree on the same meaning for a "flight arrival."

Since Delta revamped its information architecture, the company has reduced its IT costs by 30%. And despite the downturn in the airline industry, Delta has committed to a cost savings and revenue enhancement of $2 billion by the end of 2005, while increasing its service levels. Just as important, Delta has learned that discipline and simplicity in its approach to technology management lead to both speed and efficiency.

In doing the hot, sweaty work of simplifying its systems and aligning IT with the company's overarching business goals, Delta's senior managers also learned to trust their instincts. They learned that the same business skills that allowed them to see what was wrong with the company's fleet of aircraft could also guide them in managing Delta's armada of technology platforms.

Gear 3: A High-Performance IT Culture

There's no reason why most companies can't develop a long-term IT road map tied to corporate goals. There's also no reason that given sufficient discipline and resources, most can't develop a unifying IT platform. But without a high-performance IT organization in place—one that looks very different from those found in most companies—a messy IT business will persist.

For years, corporations have treated IT people differently—a holdover from "glass house" data processing culture of 30 years ago. Treating IT as if it were a separate corporate entity sets up a vicious cycle. Allowed to work in their own tribes, IT folks feel less affiliation with the company than they do with their own projects. Like the soldiers building the bridge on the River Kwai, they grow so isolated that they forget what the war is about.

By contrast, the people in a high-performance IT organization don't feel different from other corporate citizens; in fact, they are business-savvy leaders in their own right. They operate according to the same corporate values as everyone else and are measured by the same tough performance standards.

The story of the 1995 merger of Burlington Northern and Santa Fe Railroads offers a case in point. The two railroads had two very distinct cultures, performance characteristics, and leadership styles. Burlington Northern's culture was kind, collaborative, and soft on accountability. Santa Fe's culture was tough and strictly hierarchical. Thrown together into a single, 1,500-person organization, these two talented but antagonistic teams were told by CEO Rob Krebs that they had 24 months to complete a seamless merger of their separate IT systems. The goal was to develop the largest integrated, real-time rail information system in the world—one that would allow the new company to control traffic and cargo across 33,500 miles of track that covered 28 states and two Canadian provinces. From a technology standpoint, it was a challenge of immense proportions.

But once again, the issue wasn't technology; it was about establishing a new and cohesive culture, with a clear-cut set of rules and a solid performance-management and feedback system. How, the leaders asked, would people react to the deadline pressure, and how would the teams work together to accomplish a Herculean mission? How would the overhaul of systems get done? How would talent be developed?

First on the agenda was the establishment of an accountable IT leadership team. An IT organization that has clear guidance, a shared mission, and high expectations can focus the developers and engineers around the work and correct performance problems. To do so, the IT managers must be hands-on people who are deeply involved in overseeing projects and teams. In setting up a leader-led organization, BNSF established three simple levels of hierarchy: the CIO, vice presidents, and directors.

Once the new leadership structure was in place, BNSF set the performance and bonus targets for expected leadership behavior—the same ones that applied across the company as a whole. These targets had three components: delivering results, leadership competencies, and the "new BNSF" cultural behaviors. A top-performing leader had to deliver on all three of these targets. None of the IT staff members had ever been evaluated in such a clear way before, and they responded extremely well to expectations and feedback.

Part of the secret of getting people out of the old way and into the new is to establish a rhythm—that is, to control the flow, timing, and pace of the work. Setting a calendar and adhering to it is, in most cases, the most visible means of signaling the transformation of the IT culture and new set of processes. At BNSF, quarterly updates, staff meetings, directors' councils, project reviews, technical reviews, and IT board meetings all helped give the new team a sense of normality and routine—especially important for people who are undergoing a reorganization. The meetings helped transform the formerly frustrating and messy IT cultures. Instead of accepting disorganization and lack of participation as a given, people showed up on time and generally became more efficient in their jobs.

The new organization and performance system was time-consuming to put in place, of course. Most of the leaders grumbled about these demands and the intense time pressure of the work. This was especially true for those who never had to manage under a clear set of expectations. But over time, and especially with the early success of the project, healthy work patterns began to emerge, and a new culture was born. Within a few months, BNSF's newly merged IT group became a high-performance organization—so much so that it beat the 24-month target by three months. The reorganization, combined with the savings realized from streamlining processes and facilities, allowed BNSF to achieve roughly $500 million worth of cost savings that it had committed to the Interstate Commerce Commission to obtain merger approval. Without the performance gear at high torque, BNSF could not have attained its corporate goals.

All Systems Go

Once these three gears are aligned and locked together, IT organizations and systems tend to deliver results rapidly—in many cases within six months. Yet despite the obvious benefits of these gears, some businesspeople may ask themselves, "Do we really have to do all of this ourselves? Can't we simply outsource to firms that already know how to do this stuff? And wouldn't outsourcing be a cheaper alternative in the long run?"

The answer to all these questions is yes and no. Over time, fewer and fewer CIOs will run their own networks and data centers, and much development may be augmented by partners. However, the "gears" become even more critical when you bring outsourcing and offshoring into the picture, because management complexity rises. You can't abdicate the leadership and vision for these critical functions. And when you have a number of long-term contracts with various suppliers, the long-term plan must be extremely well articulated (Gear 1). When you work with a number of vendors that have their own tools and methodologies, it's critical to orchestrate an overarching common framework under which everyone can work productively (Gear 2). It's also much easier to build a high-performance culture when you own the human resources (Gear 3). In operating a multi-company workforce, it takes extraordinary leadership to create the esprit de corp required for high performance.

Without question, the next decade will require much more professional and sophisticated IT leadership than ever before. Fortunately, companies are learning fast. As we progress through the next decade, IT will mature from adolescence to adulthood, and much more speedily than any profession ever has. As the technology matures and improves, so will the skills, processes, and principles on which effective IT is based. And here's the bonus: Once organizations get IT right, they will get much more for far less.

CHARLIE S. FELD is the chairman of the Feld Group, an IT operations firm in Irving, Texas. **DONNA B. STODDARD** chairs the technology, operations, and information management division at Babson College in Massachusetts.

Originally published in February 2004. Reprint R0402E

IT Doesn't Matter

by Nicholas G. Carr

IN 1968, A YOUNG INTEL engineer named Ted Hoff found a way to put the circuits necessary for computer processing onto a tiny piece of silicon. His invention of the microprocessor spurred a series of technological breakthroughs—desktop computers, local and wide area networks, enterprise software, and the Internet—that have transformed the business world. Today, no one would dispute that information technology has become the backbone of commerce. It underpins the operations of individual companies, ties together far-flung supply chains, and, increasingly, links businesses to the customers they serve. Hardly a dollar or a euro changes hands anymore without the aid of computer systems.

As IT's power and presence have expanded, companies have come to view it as a resource ever more critical to their success, a fact clearly reflected in their spending habits. In 1965, according to a study by the U.S. Department of Commerce's Bureau of Economic Analysis, less than 5% of the capital expenditures of American companies went to information technology. After the introduction of the personal computer in the early 1980s, that percentage rose to 15%. By the early 1990s, it had reached more than 30%, and by the end of the decade it had hit nearly 50%. Even with the recent sluggishness in technology spending, businesses around the world continue to spend well over $2 trillion a year on IT.

But the veneration of IT goes much deeper than dollars. It is evident as well in the shifting attitudes of top managers. Twenty years ago, most executives looked down on computers as proletarian tools—glorified typewriters and calculators—best relegated to low-level employees like secretaries, analysts, and technicians. It was the rare executive who would let his fingers touch a keyboard, much less incorporate information technology into his strategic thinking. Today, that has changed completely. Chief executives now routinely talk about the strategic value of information technology, about how they can use IT to gain a competitive edge, about the "digitization" of their business models. Most have appointed chief information officers to their senior management teams, and many have hired strategy consulting firms to provide fresh ideas on how to leverage their IT investments for differentiation and advantage.

Behind the change in thinking lies a simple assumption: that as IT's potency and ubiquity have increased, so too has its strategic value. It's a reasonable assumption, even an intuitive one. But it's mistaken. What makes a resource truly strategic—what gives it the capacity to be the basis for a sustained competitive advantage—is not ubiquity but scarcity. You only gain

Idea in Brief

To beat your competitors, are you devoting more than 50% of your capital expenditures to information technology? If so, you're not alone. Businesses worldwide pump $2 trillion a year into IT. But like many broadly adopted technologies—such as railways and electrical power—IT has become a commodity. Affordable and accessible to everyone, it no longer offers strategic value to anyone.

Scarcity—not ubiquity—makes a business resource truly strategic. Companies gain an edge by having or doing something others can't have or do. In IT's earlier days, forward-looking firms trumped competitors through innovative deployment of IT; for example, Federal Express's package-tracking system and American Airlines' Sabre reservation system.

Now that IT is ubiquitous, however, we must focus on its risks more than its potential strategic advantages. Consider electricity. No company builds its strategy on its electrical usage—but even a brief lapse in supply can be devastating. Today, an IT disruption can prove equally paralyzing to your company's ability to make products, deliver services, and satisfy customers.

But the greatest IT risk is overspending—putting your company at a cost disadvantage. The lesson? Make IT management boring. Instead of aggressively seeking an edge through IT, manage IT's costs and risks with a frugal hand and pragmatic eye—despite any renewed hype about its strategic value. Worrying about what might go wrong isn't glamorous, but it's smart business now.

an edge over rivals by having or doing something that they can't have or do. By now, the core functions of IT—data storage, data processing, and data transport—have become available and affordable to all.[1] Their very power and presence have begun to transform them from potentially strategic resources into commodity factors of production. They are becoming costs of doing business that must be paid by all but provide distinction to none.

Idea in Practice

To avoid overinvesting in IT:

Spend Less. Rigorously evaluate expected returns from IT investments. Separate essential investments from discretionary, unnecessary, or counterproductive ones. Explore simpler and cheaper alternatives, and eliminate waste.

Example: Businesses buy 100 million+ PCs annually—yet most workers use PCs for simple applications that require a fraction of their computing power. Start imposing hard limits on upgrade costs—rather than buying new computers and applications every time suppliers roll out new features. Negotiate contracts ensuring long-term usefulness of your PC investments. If vendors balk, explore cheaper solutions, including bare-bones network PCs.

Also assess your data storage, which accounts for 50%+ of many companies' IT expenditures—even though most saved data

IT is best seen as the latest in a series of broadly adopted technologies that have reshaped industry over the past two centuries—from the steam engine and the railroad to the telegraph and the telephone to the electric generator and the internal combustion engine. For a brief period, as they were being built into the infrastructure of commerce, all these technologies opened opportunities for forward-looking companies to gain real advantages. But as their availability increased and their cost decreased—as they became ubiquitous—they became commodity inputs. From a strategic standpoint, they became invisible; they no longer mattered. That is exactly what is happening to information technology today, and the implications for corporate IT management are profound.

consists of employees' e-mails and files that have little relevance to making products or serving customers.

Follow, Don't Lead. Delay IT investments to significantly cut costs *and* decrease your risk of buying flawed or soon-to-be obsolete equipment or applications. Today, smart IT users hang back from the cutting edge, buying only after standards and best practices solidify. They let more impatient rivals shoulder the high costs of experimentation. Then they sweep past them, paying less while getting more.

Focus on Risks, Not Opportunities. Many corporations are ceding control over their IT applications and networks to vendors and other third parties. The consequences of moving from tightly controlled, proprietary systems to open, shared ones? More and more threats in the form of technical glitches, service outages, and security breaches. Focus IT resources on preparing for such disruptions—not deploying IT in radical new ways.

Vanishing Advantage

Many commentators have drawn parallels between the expansion of IT, particularly the Internet, and the rollouts of earlier technologies. Most of the comparisons, though, have focused on either the investment pattern associated with the technologies—the boom-to-bust cycle—or the technologies' roles in reshaping the operations of entire industries or even economies. Little has been said about the way the technologies influence, or fail to influence, competition at the firm level. Yet it is here that history offers some of its most important lessons to managers.

A distinction needs to be made between proprietary technologies and what might be called infrastructural technologies. Proprietary technologies can be owned, actually or effectively, by a single company. A pharmaceutical firm, for example, may hold a patent on a particular compound that serves as the basis for a family of drugs. An industrial manufacturer may discover an innovative way to employ a process technology that competitors find hard to replicate. A company that produces consumer goods may acquire exclusive rights to a new packaging material that gives its product a longer shelf life than competing brands. As long as they remain protected, proprietary technologies can be the foundations for long-term strategic advantages, enabling companies to reap higher profits than their rivals.

Infrastructural technologies, in contrast, offer far more value when shared than when used in isolation. Imagine yourself in the early nineteenth century, and suppose that one manufacturing company held the rights to all the technology required to create a railroad. If it wanted to, that company could just build proprietary lines between its suppliers, its factories, and its distributors and run its own locomotives and railcars on the tracks. And it might well operate more efficiently as a result. But, for the broader economy, the value produced by such an arrangement would be trivial compared with the value that would be produced by building an open rail network connecting many companies and many buyers. The characteristics and economics of infrastructural technologies, whether railroads or telegraph lines or power generators, make it inevitable that they will be broadly shared—that they will become part of the general business infrastructure.

In the earliest phases of its buildout, however, an infrastructural technology can take the form of a proprietary technology. As long as access to the technology is restricted—through physical limitations, intellectual property rights, high costs, or a lack of standards—a company can use it to gain advantages over rivals. Consider the period between the construction of the first electric power stations, around 1880, and the wiring of the electric grid early in the twentieth century. Electricity remained a scarce resource during this time, and those manufacturers able to tap into it—by, for example, building their plants near generating stations—often gained an important edge. It was no coincidence that the largest U.S. manufacturer of nuts and bolts at the turn of the century, Plumb, Burdict, and Barnard, located its factory near Niagara Falls in New York, the site of one of the earliest large-scale hydroelectric power plants.

Companies can also steal a march on their competitors by having superior insight into the use of a new technology. The introduction of electric power again provides a good example. Until the end of the nineteenth century, most manufacturers relied on water pressure or steam to operate their machinery. Power in those days came from a single, fixed source—a water-wheel at the side of a mill, for instance—and required an elaborate system of pulleys and gears to distribute it to individual workstations throughout the plant. When electric generators first became available, many manufacturers simply adopted them as a replacement single-point source, using them to power the existing system of pulleys and gears. Smart manufacturers, however, saw that one of the great advantages of electric power is that it is easily distributable—that it can be brought directly to workstations. By wiring their plants and installing electric motors in their machines, they were able to dispense with the cumbersome, inflexible, and costly gearing systems, gaining an important efficiency advantage over their slower-moving competitors.

In addition to enabling new, more efficient operating methods, infrastructural technologies often lead to broader market changes. Here, too, a company that sees what's coming can gain a step on myopic rivals. In the mid-1800s, when America started to lay down rail lines in earnest, it was already possible to transport goods over long distances—hundreds of steamships plied the country's rivers. Businessmen probably assumed that rail transport would essentially follow the steamship model, with some incremental enhancements. In fact, the greater speed, capacity, and reach of the railroads fundamentally changed the structure of American industry. It suddenly became economical to ship finished products, rather than just raw materials and industrial components, over great distances, and the mass consumer market came into being. Companies that were quick to recognize the broader opportunity rushed to build large-scale, mass-production factories. The resulting economies of scale allowed them to crush the small, local plants that until then had dominated manufacturing.

The trap that executives often fall into, however, is assuming that opportunities for advantage will be available indefinitely. In actuality, the window for gaining advantage from an infrastructural technology is open only briefly. When the technology's commercial potential begins to be broadly appreciated, huge amounts of cash are inevitably invested in it, and its buildout proceeds with extreme speed. Railroad tracks, telegraph wires, power lines—all were laid or strung in a frenzy of activity (a frenzy so intense in the case of rail lines that it cost hundreds of laborers their lives). In the 30 years between 1846 and 1876, reports Eric Hobsbawm in *The Age of Capital,* the world's total rail trackage increased from 17,424 kilometers to 309,641 kilometers. During this same period, total steamship tonnage also exploded, from 139,973 to 3,293,072 tons. The telegraph system spread even more swiftly. In Continental Europe, there were just 2,000 miles of telegraph wires in 1849; 20 years later, there were 110,000. The pattern continued with electrical power. The number of central stations operated by utilities grew from 468 in 1889 to 4,364 in 1917, and the average capacity of each increased more than tenfold. (For a discussion of the dangers of overinvestment, see the sidebar "Too Much of a Good Thing.")

By the end of the buildout phase, the opportunities for individual advantage are largely gone. The rush to invest leads to more competition, greater capacity, and falling prices, making the technology broadly accessible and affordable. At the same time, the buildout forces users to adopt universal technical standards, rendering proprietary systems obsolete. Even the way the technology is used begins to become standardized, as best

Too Much of a Good Thing

AS MANY EXPERTS HAVE POINTED out, the overinvestment in information technology in the 1990s echoes the overinvestment in railroads in the 1860s. In both cases, companies and individuals, dazzled by the seemingly unlimited commercial possibilities of the technologies, threw large quantities of money away on half-baked businesses and products. Even worse, the flood of capital led to enormous overcapacity, devastating entire industries.

We can only hope that the analogy ends there. The mid-nineteenth-century boom in railroads (and the closely related technologies of the steam engine and the telegraph) helped produce not only wide-spread industrial overcapacity but a surge in productivity. The combination set the stage for two solid decades of deflation. Although worldwide economic production continued to grow strongly between the mid-1870s and the mid-1890s, prices collapsed—in England, the dominant economic power of the time, price levels dropped 40%. In turn, business profits evaporated. Companies watched the value of their products erode while they were in the very process of making them. As the first worldwide depression took hold, economic malaise covered much of the globe. "Optimism about a future of indefinite progress gave way to uncertainty and a sense of agony," wrote historian D. S. Landes.

It's a very different world today, of course, and it would be dangerous to assume that history will repeat itself. But with companies struggling to boost profits and the entire world economy flirting with deflation, it would also be dangerous to assume it can't.

---

practices come to be widely understood and emulated. Often, in fact, the best practices end up being built into the infrastructure itself; after electrification, for example, all new factories were constructed with many well-distributed power outlets. Both the technology and its modes of use become, in effect, commoditized. The only meaningful advantage most companies can hope to gain from an infrastructural technology after its buildout is a cost advantage—and even that tends to be very hard to sustain.

That's not to say that infrastructural technologies don't continue to influence competition. They do, but their influence is felt at the macroeconomic level, not at the level of the individual company. If a particular country, for instance, lags in installing the technology—whether it's a national rail network, a power grid, or a communication infrastructure—its domestic industries will suffer heavily. Similarly, if an industry lags in harnessing the power of the technology, it will be vulnerable to displacement. As always, a company's fate is tied to broader forces affecting its region and its industry. The point is, however, that the technology's potential for differentiating one company from the pack—its strategic potential—inexorably declines as it becomes accessible and affordable to all.

The Commoditization of IT

Although more complex and malleable than its predecessors, IT has all the hallmarks of an infrastructural technology. In fact, its mix of characteristics guarantees particularly rapid commoditization. IT is, first of all, a transport mechanism—it carries digital information just as railroads carry goods and power grids carry electricity. And like any transport mechanism, it is far more valuable when shared than when used in isolation. The history of IT in business has been a history of increased

What About the Vendors?

JUST A FEW MONTHS AGO, at the 2003 World Economic Forum in Davos, Switzerland, Bill Joy, the chief scientist and cofounder of Sun Microsystems, posed what for him must have been a painful question: "What if the reality is that people have already bought most of the stuff they want to own?" The people he was talking about are, of course, businesspeople, and the stuff is information technology. With the end of the great buildout of the commercial IT infrastructure apparently at hand, Joy's question is one that all IT vendors should be asking themselves. There is good reason to believe that companies' existing IT capabilities are largely sufficient for their needs and, hence, that the recent and widespread sluggishness in IT demand is as much a structural as a cyclical phenomenon.

Even if that's true, the picture may not be as bleak as it seems for vendors, at least those with the foresight and skill to adapt to the new environment. The importance of infrastructural technologies to the day-to-day operations of business means that they continue to absorb large amounts of corporate cash long after they have become commodities—indefinitely, in many cases. Virtually all companies today continue to spend heavily on electricity and phone service, for example, and many manufacturers continue to spend

interconnectivity and interoperability, from mainframe time-sharing to minicomputer-based local area networks to broader Ethernet networks and on to the Internet. Each stage in that progression has involved greater standardization of the technology and, at least recently, greater homogenization of its functionality. For most business applications today, the benefits of customization would be overwhelmed by the costs of isolation.

IT is also highly replicable. Indeed, it is hard to imagine a more perfect commodity than a byte of data—endlessly and perfectly reproducible at virtually no cost.

a lot on rail transport. Moreover, the standardized nature of infrastructural technologies often leads to the establishment of lucrative monopolies and oligopolies.

Many technology vendors are already repositioning themselves and their products in response to the changes in the market. Microsoft's push to turn its Office software suite from a packaged good into an annual subscription service is a tacit acknowledgment that companies are losing their need—and their appetite—for constant upgrades. Dell has succeeded by exploiting the commoditization of the PC market and is now extending that strategy to servers, storage, and even services. (Michael Dell's essential genius has always been his unsentimental trust in the commoditization of information technology.) And many of the major suppliers of corporate IT, including Microsoft, IBM, Sun, and Oracle, are battling to position themselves as dominant suppliers of "Web services"—to turn themselves, in effect, into utilities. This war for scale, combined with the continuing transformation of IT into a commodity, will lead to the further consolidation of many sectors of the IT industry. The winners will do very well; the losers will be gone.

The near-infinite scalability of many IT functions, when combined with technical standardization, dooms most proprietary applications to economic obsolescence. Why write your own application for word processing or e-mail or, for that matter, supply-chain management when you can buy a ready-made, state-of-the-art application for a fraction of the cost? But it's not just the software that is replicable. Because most business activities and processes have come to be embedded in software, they become replicable, too. When companies buy a generic application, they buy a generic process as well.

Both the cost savings and the interoperability benefits make the sacrifice of distinctiveness unavoidable.

The arrival of the Internet has accelerated the commoditization of IT by providing a perfect delivery channel for generic applications. More and more, companies will fulfill their IT requirements simply by purchasing fee-based "Web services" from third parties—similar to the way they currently buy electric power or telecommunications services. Most of the major business-technology vendors, from Microsoft to IBM, are trying to position themselves as IT utilities, companies that will control the provision of a diverse range of business applications over what is now called, tellingly, "the grid." Again, the upshot is ever greater homogenization of IT capabilities, as more companies replace customized applications with generic ones. (For more on the challenges facing IT companies, see the sidebar "What About the Vendors?")

Finally, and for all the reasons already discussed, IT is subject to rapid price deflation. When Gordon Moore made his famously prescient assertion that the density of circuits on a computer chip would double every two years, he was making a prediction about the coming explosion in processing power. But he was also making a prediction about the coming free fall in the price of computer functionality. The cost of processing power has dropped relentlessly, from $480 per million instructions per second (MIPS) in 1978 to $50 per MIPS in 1985 to $4 per MIPS in 1995, a trend that continues unabated. Similar declines have occurred in the cost of data storage and transmission. The rapidly increasing affordability of IT functionality has not only democratized the computer revolution, it has destroyed one of the most important potential barriers to competitors. Even the most cutting-edge IT capabilities quickly become available to all.

It's no surprise, given these characteristics, that IT's evolution has closely mirrored that of earlier infrastructural technologies. Its buildout has been every bit as breathtaking as that of the railroads (albeit with considerably fewer fatalities). Consider some statistics. During the last quarter of the twentieth century, the computational power of a microprocessor increased by a factor of 66,000. In the dozen years from 1989 to 2001, the number of host computers connected to the Internet grew from 80,000 to more than 125 million. Over the last ten years, the number of sites on the World Wide Web has grown from zero to nearly 40 million. And since the 1980s, more than 280 million miles of fiber-optic cable have been installed—enough, as *BusinessWeek* recently noted, to "circle the earth 11,320 times." (See the exhibit "The Sprint to Commoditization.")

As with earlier infrastructural technologies, IT provided forward-looking companies many opportunities for competitive advantage early in its buildout, when it could still be "owned" like a proprietary technology. A classic example is American Hospital Supply. A leading distributor of medical supplies, AHS introduced in 1976 an innovative system called Analytic Systems Automated Purchasing, or ASAP, that enabled hospitals to order goods electronically. Developed in-house, the innovative system used proprietary software running on a mainframe computer, and hospital purchasing agents

The sprint to commoditization

One of the most salient characteristics of infrastructural technologies is the rapidity of their installation. Spurred by massive investment, capacity soon skyrockets, leading to falling prices and, quickly, commoditization.

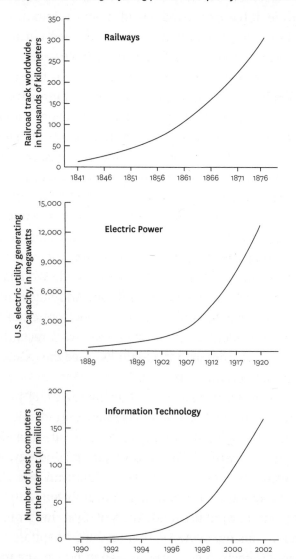

Sources: railways: Eric Hobsbawm, *The Age of Capital* (Vintage, 1996); electric power: Richard B. Duboff, *Electric Power in Manufacturing, 1889–1958* (Arno, 1979); Internet hosts: Robert H. Zakon, *Hobbes' Internet Timeline* (www.zakon.org/robert/internet/timeline/).

accessed it through terminals at their sites. Because more efficient ordering enabled hospitals to reduce their inventories—and thus their costs—customers were quick to embrace the system. And because it was proprietary to AHS, it effectively locked out competitors. For several years, in fact, AHS was the only distributor offering electronic ordering, a competitive advantage that led to years of superior financial results. From 1978 to 1983, AHS's sales and profits rose at annual rates of 13% and 18%, respectively—well above industry averages.

AHS gained a true competitive advantage by capitalizing on characteristics of infrastructural technologies that are common in the early stages of their buildouts, in particular their high cost and lack of standardization. Within a decade, however, those barriers to competition were crumbling. The arrival of personal computers and packaged software, together with the emergence of networking standards, was rendering proprietary communication systems unattractive to their users and uneconomical to their owners. Indeed, in an ironic, if predictable, twist, the closed nature and outdated technology of AHS's system turned it from an asset to a liability. By the dawn of the 1990s, after AHS had merged with Baxter Travenol to form Baxter International, the company's senior executives had come to view ASAP as "a millstone around their necks," according to a Harvard Business School case study.

Myriad other companies have gained important advantages through the innovative deployment of IT. Some, like American Airlines with its Sabre reservation system, Federal Express with its package-tracking system, and Mobil Oil with its automated Speedpass payment system, used IT to gain particular operating or marketing advantages—to leapfrog the competition in one process or activity. Others, like Reuters with its 1970s financial information network or, more recently, eBay with its Internet auctions, had superior insight into the way IT would fundamentally change an industry and were able to stake out commanding positions. In a few cases, the dominance companies gained through IT innovation conferred additional advantages, such as scale economies and brand recognition, that have proved more durable than the original technological edge. Wal-Mart and Dell Computer are renowned examples of firms that have been able to turn temporary technological advantages into enduring positioning advantages.

But the opportunities for gaining IT-based advantages are already dwindling. Best practices are now quickly built into software or otherwise replicated. And as for IT-spurred industry transformations, most of the ones that are going to happen have likely already happened or are in the process of happening. Industries and markets will continue to evolve, of course, and some will undergo fundamental changes—the future of the music business, for example, continues to be in doubt. But history shows that the power of an infrastructural technology to transform industries always diminishes as its buildout nears completion.

While no one can say precisely when the buildout of an infrastructural technology has concluded, there are many signs that the IT buildout is much closer to its end than its beginning. First, IT's power is outstripping most of the business needs it fulfills. Second, the price of essential IT functionality has dropped to the point where it is more or less affordable to all. Third, the capacity of the universal distribution network (the Internet) has caught up with demand—indeed, we already have considerably more fiber-optic capacity than we need. Fourth, IT vendors are rushing to position themselves as commodity suppliers or even as utilities. Finally, and most definitively, the investment bubble has burst, which historically has been a clear indication that an infrastructural technology is reaching the end of its buildout. A few companies may still be able to wrest advantages from highly specialized applications that don't offer strong economic incentives for replication, but those firms will be the exceptions that prove the rule.

At the close of the 1990s, when Internet hype was at full boil, technologists offered grand visions of an emerging "digital future." It may well be that, in terms of business strategy at least, the future has already arrived.

From Offense to Defense

So what should companies do? From a practical standpoint, the most important lesson to be learned from earlier infrastructural technologies may be this: When a resource becomes essential to competition but inconsequential to strategy, the risks it creates become more important than the advantages it provides. Think of electricity. Today, no company builds its business strategy around its electricity usage, but even a brief lapse in supply can be devastating (as some California businesses discovered during the energy crisis of 2000). The operational risks associated with IT are many—technical glitches, obsolescence, service outages, unreliable vendors or partners, security breaches, even terrorism—and some have become magnified as companies have moved from tightly controlled, proprietary systems to open, shared ones. Today, an IT disruption can paralyze a company's ability to make its products, deliver its services, and connect with its customers, not to mention foul its reputation. Yet few companies have done a thorough job of identifying and tempering their vulnerabilities. Worrying about what might go wrong may not be as glamorous a job as speculating about the future, but it is a more essential job right now. (See the sidebar "New Rules for IT Management.")

In the long run, though, the greatest IT risk facing most companies is more prosaic than a catastrophe. It is, simply, overspending. IT may be a commodity, and its costs may fall rapidly enough to ensure that any new capabilities are quickly shared, but the very fact that it is entwined with so many business functions means that it will continue to consume a large portion of corporate spending. For most companies, just staying in business will require big outlays for IT. What's important—and this holds true for any commodity input—is to be able to separate essential investments from ones that are discretionary, unnecessary, or even counterproductive.

New Rules for IT Management

WITH THE OPPORTUNITIES FOR GAINING strategic advantage from information technology rapidly disappearing, many companies will want to take a hard look at how they invest in IT and manage their systems. As a starting point, here are three guidelines for the future:

Spend less. Studies show that the companies with the biggest IT investments rarely post the best financial results. As the commoditization of IT continues, the penalties for wasteful spending will only grow larger. It is getting much harder to achieve a competitive advantage through an IT investment, but it is getting much easier to put your business at a cost disadvantage.

Follow, don't lead. Moore's Law guarantees that the longer you wait to make an IT purchase, the more you'll get for your money. And waiting will decrease your risk of buying something technologically flawed or doomed to rapid obsolescence. In some cases, being on the cutting edge makes sense. But those cases are becoming rarer and rarer as IT capabilities become more homogenized.

Focus on vulnerabilities, not opportunities. It's unusual for a company to gain a competitive advantage through the distinctive use of a mature infrastructural technology, but even a brief disruption in the availability of the technology can be devastating. As corporations continue to cede control over their IT applications and networks to vendors and other third parties, the threats they face will proliferate. They need to prepare themselves for technical glitches, outages, and security breaches, shifting their attention from opportunities to vulnerabilities.

At a high level, stronger cost management requires more rigor in evaluating expected returns from systems investments, more creativity in exploring simpler and cheaper alternatives, and a greater openness to outsourcing and other partnerships. But most companies can also reap significant savings by simply cutting out waste. Personal computers are a good example. Every year, businesses purchase more than 100 million PCs, most of which replace older models. Yet the vast majority of workers who use PCs rely on only a few simple applications—word processing, spreadsheets, e-mail, and Web browsing. These applications have been technologically mature for years; they require only a fraction of the computing power provided by today's microprocessors. Nevertheless, companies continue to roll out across-the-board hardware and software upgrades.

Much of that spending, if truth be told, is driven by vendors' strategies. Big hardware and software suppliers have become very good at parceling out new features and capabilities in ways that force companies into buying new computers, applications, and networking equipment much more frequently than they need to. The time has come for IT buyers to throw their weight around, to negotiate contracts that ensure the long-term usefulness of their PC investments and impose hard limits on upgrade costs. And if vendors balk, companies should be willing to explore cheaper solutions, including open-source applications and bare-bones network PCs, even if it means sacrificing features. If a company needs evidence of the kind of money that might be saved, it need only look at Microsoft's profit margin.

In addition to being passive in their purchasing, companies have been sloppy in their use of IT. That's particularly true with data storage, which has come to account for more than half of many companies' IT expenditures. The bulk of what's being stored on corporate networks has little to do with making products or serving customers—it consists of employees' saved e-mails and files, including terabytes of spam, MP3s, and video clips. *Computerworld* estimates that as much as 70% of the storage capacity of a typical Windows network is wasted—an enormous unnecessary expense. Restricting employees' ability to save files indiscriminately and indefinitely may seem distasteful to many managers, but it can have a real impact on the bottom line. Now that IT has become the dominant capital expense for most businesses, there's no excuse for waste and sloppiness.

Given the rapid pace of technology's advance, delaying IT investments can be another powerful way to cut costs—while also reducing a firm's chance of being saddled with buggy or soon-to-be-obsolete technology. Many companies, particularly during the 1990s, rushed their IT investments either because they hoped to capture a first-mover advantage or because they feared being left behind. Except in very rare cases, both the hope and the fear were unwarranted. The smartest users of technology—here again, Dell and Wal-Mart stand out—stay well back from the cutting edge, waiting to make purchases until standards and best practices solidify. They let their impatient competitors shoulder the high costs of experimentation, and then they sweep past them, spending less and getting more.

Some managers may worry that being stingy with IT dollars will damage their competitive positions. But studies of corporate IT spending consistently show that greater expenditures rarely translate into superior financial results. In fact, the opposite is usually true. In 2002, the consulting firm Alinean compared the IT expenditures and the financial results of 7,500 large U.S. companies and discovered that the top performers tended to be among the most tightfisted. The 25 companies that delivered the highest economic returns, for example, spent on average just 0.8% of their revenues on IT, while the typical company spent 3.7%. A recent study by Forrester Research showed, similarly, that the most lavish spenders on IT rarely post the best results. Even Oracle's Larry Ellison, one of the great technology salesmen, admitted in a recent interview that "most companies spend too much [on IT] and get very little in return." As the opportunities for IT-based advantage continue to narrow, the penalties for overspending will only grow.

IT management should, frankly, become boring. The key to success, for the vast majority of companies, is no longer to seek advantage aggressively but to manage costs and risks meticulously. If, like many executives, you've begun to take a more defensive posture toward IT in the last two years, spending more frugally and thinking more pragmatically, you're already on the right course. The challenge will be to maintain that discipline when the business cycle strengthens and the chorus of hype about IT's strategic value rises anew.

Note

1. "Information technology" is a fuzzy term. In this article, it is used in its common current sense, as denoting the technologies used for processing, storing, and transporting information in digital form.

NICHOLAS G. CARR, formerly HBR's editor-at-large, writes about technology, business, and culture.

Originally published in May 2003. Reprint R0305B

Bold Retreat

A New Strategy for Old Technologies
by Ron Adner and Daniel C. Snow

A SUPERIOR NEW TECHNOLOGY emerges on the horizon, threatening your existing business. Do you simply follow conventional wisdom and strive to make a seamless transition to the new technology? All too many companies can't admit to themselves that they actually don't have the wherewithal to make that transition—and so they fail disastrously.

Some firms decide, of course, that they can't or shouldn't make the transition—perhaps because they lack the necessary capabilities or financial resources, or because they believe that the new technology isn't really superior and can be defeated. So, they redouble their efforts to upgrade the old technology and in many cases succeed in improving its performance. For example, manufacturers of electric typewriters responded to the rise of digital word processors by making mass-market machines that were performance wonders, with spell checking, full-line erasing, and multiple fonts. Chemical-film photography firms responded to the rise of digital cameras by developing the Advanced Photo System (APS), which improved print quality and introduced new features, such as multiple picture formats and index prints, in a new cartridge-based format.

However, such last gasps usually only postpone the day of reckoning. The superior technology almost always wins in the end. Managers of old-technology firms who try to delay the inevitable often waste resources and damage their companies.

In studying the history of technology transitions, we have discovered that companies that depend on a mature technology have a third option when a new technology emerges: They can retreat to a defensible niche, where the old technology has an advantage. Long after their technologies were eclipsed in their core markets, these firms still prosper. Linjett continues to succeed with leisure sailboats despite the dominance of marine engine power. Continental maintains its business in piston engines for private aircraft despite the dominance of jet turbine power in commercial aviation. And StorageTek has found a profitable niche for its magnetic-tape-drive technology—large-scale data archives—that it can successfully defend from the disk-drive technology that has come to dominate the mainstream computer-storage market.

These firms engaged in what we call a *bold retreat*. The strategy is a retreat because the firm cedes most of the established market to the new, dominant technology and instead pursues less vulnerable positions. And it's bold because the withdrawal is a proactive, strategic alternative to head-on competition with the

Idea in Brief

A superior new technology emerges on the horizon, threatening your existing business. Do you strive to make a seamless transition to it or, perhaps, try to fight and defeat it? Both of those responses can be losing strategies. A third, frequently superior, option is one of "bold retreat," whereby your company cedes most of the established market to the new, dominant technology and instead pursues less vulnerable positions—not as a "turn tail and run" reaction but as a proactive, strategic alternative to head-on competition. There are two types of bold retreats: (1) retrenchment to a niche of the traditional market, where the old technology has an advantage over the new one in addressing customer needs; and (2) relocation to a new market, where the old technology is the inherently superior offering. You can even incorporate both moves into an effective strategy. Like a transition to a new technology, a bold retreat requires significant organizational change. That includes revamping your cost structure and talent base, not to mention selling the very idea of "retreat" to your internal stakeholders. Despite such challenges, a bold retreat that is carried out with foresight can be both a survival strategy and a success story.

new technology. Linjett, Continental, and StorageTek extended the value of their competence base by transforming their market position; they retrenched within sustainable niches of their traditional markets, relocated to other markets where the old technology might actually have an advantage, or both.

A bold retreat should be considered routinely along with the more conventional strategy options. It can help save managers from making an overly risky bet that their company will be able to defeat, or make the leap to, a new technology. Or, if a company can realistically pull off a transition, a bold retreat can help finance the move. In recessionary times, profitably extending the lives of old technologies is especially important.

Openly discussing a retreat is rarely easy or intuitive for managers, in large part because it runs counter to the notion that exemplary business leaders vanquish their competitors and grow their companies. And to be sure, retreat is not always the best choice. It is, however, almost always a *relevant* option. Firms that lack a structured process for considering retreat are unwisely excluding a valuable strategic alternative. In this article, we examine how to recognize when a retrenchment to a niche within your traditional market or a relocation to a new market makes sense, and we discuss some organizational challenges to executing such moves.

Retrenching to Sustainable Niches

A new technology does more than just present more competition for an old technology. It presents a different type of competition whose value proposition does not fully overlap with the old-technology offer. So, instead of focusing on how to catch up in the overlapping areas, you can ask, "What has been left unaddressed? What has the new technology revealed about our offer that we could not see without it?"

Consider watches. Before 1969, a watch was just a watch. There were expensive watches, inexpensive watches, manual and automatic-winding watches, calendar watches, and many other categories that customers bought. All were powered by mechanical-movement systems, and a key measure of performance was accuracy. In 1969, quartz watches were introduced. They offered an order-of-magnitude increase in accuracy—and at a much lower cost. Within a decade of its introduction, quartz movement became the dominant watch technology. Mechanical-watch makers faced two obvious but unattractive options: Attempt a highly uncertain transition to produce quartz movement (even though they had little relevant competence in that technology) or redouble efforts to improve the price and performance of their mechanical-movement devices, thereby merely narrowing, but not closing, the performance gap with quartz.

Insightful firms, however, recognized a third option. They realized that the rise of the quartz movement meant that for the first time, consumers could choose between mechanical and nonmechanical watches. Or, to put it another way, the introduction of nonmechanical watches made some consumers aware of their preference for "mechanicalness." These watchmakers began redesigning their products with this segment in mind. One result was a shift from the industry norm of hiding watch mechanisms within an opaque case to making parts of the case transparent in order to show off the increasingly complicated, visually stimulating mechanical movements.

Clearly, the niche of consumers who valued the mechanical quality of a watch was smaller than the broader watch market. However, these consumers were willing to pay a high price. And perhaps more important, this niche was immune to attack from the purveyors of quartz movement.

Such dynamics govern the survival of other old technologies, many of which do not occupy the high ends of their markets. Dot matrix printers outperform laser printers in many industrial applications, because their print heads are less sensitive to dust, vibration, and temperature changes and because they can print thick, multilayer forms. Similarly, pager networks still enjoy success in the health care and emergency-services markets because pagers do not generate transmissions that interfere with medical equipment in the way that cell phones do. In all these cases, old-technology firms found ways of leveraging the differences in performance between the old and new technologies, rather than attempting to eliminate them.

In our research, we have observed many types of retrenchment maneuvers—up-market, down-market, mid-market, and combinations of these. No simple formula works for deciding which ones are best. Managers must work to identify all the potential safe harbors, to assess the size of these opportunities and the resources required to tap them, and to determine whether they will allow the business to operate at an acceptable scale. (See the guiding questions in the sidebar "Retrenchment: Holding On to Old Segments.") If it turns out that opportunities to retrench don't exist or are too small to support the business, consider another option: finding a new market.

Relocating to a New Market

Relocation involves using the old technology to solve either a new set of problems for the same set of customers

Retrenchment: Holding On to Old Segments

USE THESE EIGHT QUESTIONS TO guide your efforts to retrench an old technology.

1. What elements of our value creation does the new technology leave unaddressed? (Think broadly—for example, about performance, mode of delivery, service interaction, and so on.)

2. Which of our customers care about these elements?

3. If we were to focus on these unique attributes, how could we further improve value creation for this customer?

4. If we could capture this segment, would it be enough to sustain us—in terms of revenues, margins, and differentiation from the competition?

5. How would we need to change our organization?

6. What can we expect in terms of competition?

7. Will our ecosystem of suppliers and complementors be available to support this move?

8. How attractive is this option relative to our realistic alternatives?

or the existing problems of a new set of customers. It means actively pursuing the new opportunities and abandoning old positions. (See the guiding questions in the sidebar "Relocation: Finding New Markets.")

If these are such good opportunities, why wouldn't a company have pursued them during the normal course of expansion, before the new technology came on the scene? The simple answer is that the new technology

Relocation: Finding New Markets

USE THESE SIX QUESTIONS TO guide your efforts to move an old technology to a new market.

1. If we gave away the old technology for free, who would want it? Who could use it?

2. Why aren't those who might want the old technology using it now?

3. What are these potential customers using instead? How much are they paying?

4. What adjustments would we need to make in order to sell at this price?

5. How much more value would this new set of customers derive if they used our technology instead of the current alternative?

6. Compared with our other choices, how attractive is the relocation option?

changes the business-development calculus for old technology: The priority of normal diversification is growth, whereas the priority of relocation is survival. So, opportunities outside the traditional market that seemed insufficiently attractive before the advent of the new technology may become a lot more appealing as opportunities in the traditional market disappear, especially if they provide a defensible refuge. For example, programmable calculators have been largely replaced by computers in business and science markets for solving complex problems, but they now thrive in the education market, where their low price and portability make them perfect for teaching standard graphing concepts.

Similarly, local pager networks are now widely used by restaurants to call patrons to their tables.

A Bold-Retreat Case Study: Ultratech

To understand how relocation and retrenchment can work in concert, consider the story of Ultratech. The company was a successful producer of 1x semiconductor lithography steppers, which help to transfer circuit designs onto silicon wafers. After a management buyout, resource constraints prevented Ultratech from following its peers in developing the next generation of 5x steppers, which used complex optics to reduce image sizes by a factor of five, thereby enhancing printing resolutions. Recognizing that 5x would soon outsell 1x technology in the core market, Ultratech's management made a bold decision: If the company couldn't afford to reinvent its technology in order to compete in its existing market, it would maintain its existing technology and reinvent its market position.

Ultratech's first move was to retrench in a lower-end segment of the semiconductor wafer market, serving less-demanding lithography procedures. This was more challenging than it sounds. To make operations simpler, chip makers had been using just one type of tool from just one supplier throughout their manufacturing line, even though many production steps did not require the most advanced performance. Without a 5x product, Ultratech knew that it couldn't compete on this basis. Instead, it broke with industry practice and targeted its 1x tools only at steps that did not require cutting-edge performance. That entailed developing technologies and processes that allowed chip makers to mix and match Ultratech's tools with those of competitors and persuading customers to alter their purchasing habits. These steps required Ultratech to orchestrate substantial organizational changes, including in development, sales, and marketing.

In addition to retrenching, Ultratech searched for relocation opportunities outside its traditional market. It identified applications that valued high-resolution printing but did not require 5x resolutions. One was the manufacture of thin-film heads for disk drives. With drive performance improving at an extremely high rate, the resolution requirements in head production were constantly increasing. Ultratech's technology offered significantly better resolution performance than the metal-in-gap technology that was being used—and at a competitive price. Although the 5x technology's performance would have been even more attractive to drive-head producers, its high price point excluded it from serving the disk-drive market.

In effect, Ultratech decided not to participate in a technology race that it was sure to lose. Instead, it boldly retreated to new markets, allowing it to regain its financial footing and then use its resources to innovate in a more promising area: laser-spike-annealing equipment, which is used in semiconductor manufacturing but does not compete with lithography. The company pioneered this technology and established itself as the market leader.

One can't help wondering if other companies that foundered when their mainstay markets were challenged by a new technology might have fared better if they, too, had proactively retreated to defensible niches. For example, Kodak might be healthier today had it reacted to the rise of digital photography by focusing on niche markets such as disposable cameras and allocating resources to more-defensible niches such as medical imaging. Instead, it fought a losing battle to extend the life of its mass-market chemical-photography business with its APS initiative. Similarly, AOL could have responded to the rise of the World Wide Web by retreating from its mass-market strategy and offering its "walled garden" to niches that valued exclusivity.

Organizing Bold Retreats

Making a transition from an old technology to a new one is, of course, extremely difficult. A lack of technical competence; radically different production, sales, and support requirements; and culture clashes between the advocates of the new and the defenders of the old are only a few of many obstacles to expect.

What may be less obvious is the significant organizational change that retrenching or relocating an old technology requires. Product-development, manufacturing, marketing, and sales priorities must all be refocused on creating the most value for the new target markets. And because retreat entails much more subtle organizational adjustments than making the leap to a new technology involves, leaders may have to play a hands-on role in managing day-to-day activities. Here are some guidelines for leading such a transition.

Revamp your organization's focus, cost structure, and talent base.
Retreats often require painful resizing to align the organization's footprint and cost structure with those that can be supported in the niche. The R&D function, for example, must shift its focus from exploring its industry's technology frontier to refining the existing technology in order to address the needs of different sets of users, which often include a new price-performance balance. Similarly, the sales and marketing functions must adjust to support a different market position with a different client base. This may require substantial changes in personnel. Indeed, the stars who excelled at finding ways to extend the old technology's performance in the mainstream market may be those least suited to finding ways to guide it away from the mainstream.

Be prepared to deal with upheaval in your ecosystem.
The emergence of a new technology inevitably causes members of the old technology's ecosystem—suppliers, complementors, distributors, and even capital providers—to reassess their roles and relationships (see "Match Your Innovation Strategy to Your Innovation Ecosystem," HBR April 2006). Some may decide to abandon their support of the old technology in order to concentrate resources on supporting the new one. Even those that can't make the transition to the new technology may decide that the opportunities offered by the repositioned old technology are inadequate and choose to exit the business. The result: a critical hole in the ecosystem that's hard to fill. For example, manufacturers of high-end audio equipment have

struggled to find sources of vacuum tubes. If critical partners abandon the old technology, your firm may have to perform that role itself.

Appreciate the risks of embracing a mixed (old + new) strategy.

Deciding whether to embrace an emerging new technology or reposition the old one is not necessarily an either-or decision. Indeed, at first glance there are advantages to attempting both: potential synergies and spillovers, shared learning, maximized return on investment in the old technology, and so on. In reality, these benefits are difficult to realize. Getting the team that's pursuing the new technology and the team that's extending the life of the old one to share resources and capabilities is easier said than done, especially when teams find themselves competing for customers. By being extremely explicit about ground rules such as which market segments the old technology will not compete for, management can reduce internal conflicts and optimize the performance of both teams.

Remember the competition.

It's highly likely that a smaller target market will be able to support only a smaller number of rivals. Preempting competitors by moving early into a niche may be crucial.

Don't underestimate the challenges of selling a retreat strategy.

Militaries have long regarded retreat as a legitimate—and responsible—strategic option. Not so in business.

Most executives rise to the top of their organizations by promising and delivering growth, success, and better times. Giving up a market position without a big fight runs counter to the can-do attitude that we expect from business leaders. Although it's easy to get your organization, including your board of directors, to understand why a retreat is necessary after the business has suffered deep losses, it is much harder to successfully argue for retreat before the battle has begun. Do not allow accusations of timidity to overwhelm the logic of realistic foresight.

A bold technology retreat is not always a viable option, let alone an optimal one, when a new technology emerges. However, it's an option that must be considered during a strategic review. Retreating to an existing niche or relocating to a new market may allow a firm to continue to prosper on a more modest scale. These positions can serve as a safe haven for recouping strength and then attacking new growth opportunities.

In all cases, however, retreats have to be bold. They must be pursued before the technology fight is lost and the firm's resources are drained—and before the advancing new technology has taken hold and created a crisis for your business. Retreats carried out proactively can avert catastrophic defeats.

RON ADNER is an associate professor in the strategy and management department at the Tuck School of Business at Dartmouth College. **DANIEL C. SNOW** is an assistant professor in the technology and operations management unit at Harvard Business School.

Originally published in March 2010. Reprint R1003E

Information Technology and the Board of Directors

by Richard Nolan and F. Warren McFarlan

EVER SINCE THE Y2K SCARE, boards have grown increasingly nervous about corporate dependence on information technology. Since then, computer crashes, denial of service attacks, competitive pressures, and the need to automate compliance with government regulations have heightened board sensitivity to IT risk. Unfortunately, most boards remain largely in the dark when it comes to IT spending and strategy. Despite the fact that corporate information assets can account for more than 50% of capital spending, most boards fall into the default mode of applying a set of tacit or explicit rules cobbled together from the best practices of other firms. Few understand the full degree of their operational dependence on computer systems or the extent to which IT plays a role in shaping their firms' strategies.

This state of affairs may seem excusable because to date there have been no standards for IT governance. Certainly, board committees understand their roles with regard to other areas of corporate control. In the U.S., the audit committee's task, for example, is codified in a set of Generally Accepted Accounting Principles and processes, and underscored by regulations such as those of the New York Stock Exchange and Securities and Exchange Commission. Likewise, the compensation committee acts according to generally understood principles, employing compensation consulting firms to verify its findings and help explain its decisions to shareholders. The governance committee, too, has a clear mission: to look at the composition of the board and recommend improvements to its processes. To be sure, boards often fail to reach set standards, but at least there are standards.

Because there has been no comparable body of knowledge and best practice, IT governance doesn't exist per se. Indeed, board members frequently lack the fundamental knowledge needed to ask intelligent questions about not only IT risk and expense but also competitive risk. This leaves the CIOs, who manage critical corporate information assets, pretty much on their own. A lack of board oversight for IT activities is dangerous; it puts the firm at risk in the same way that failing to audit its books would.

Understanding this, a small group of companies has taken matters into its own hands and established rigorous IT governance committees. Mellon Financial, Novell, Home Depot, Procter & Gamble, Wal-Mart, and

Idea in Brief

Ever since the Y2K scare, boards have grown increasingly nervous about corporate dependence on information technology. Since then, computer crashes, denial of service attacks, competitive pressures, and the need to automate compliance with government regulations have heightened board sensitivity to IT risk. Unfortunately, most boards remain largely in the dark when it comes to IT spending and strategy, despite the fact that corporate information assets can account for more than 50% of capital spending. A lack of board oversight for IT activities is dangerous, the authors say. It puts firms at risk in the same way that failing to audit their books would. Companies that have established board-level IT governance committees are better able to control IT project costs and carve out competitive advantage. But there is no one-size-fits-all model for board supervision of a company's IT operations. The correct approach depends on what strategic "mode" a company is in—whether its operations are extremely dependent on IT and whether it relies heavily on keeping up with the latest technologies. This article spells out the conditions under which boards need to change their level of involvement in IT decisions, explaining how members can recognize their firms' IT risks and decide whether they should pursue more aggressive IT governance. The authors delineate what an IT governance committee should look like in terms of charter, membership, duties, and overall agenda. They also offer recommendations for developing IT policies that take into account an organization's operational and strategic needs, and suggest what to do when those needs change. Given the dizzying pace of change in the world of IT, boards can't afford to ignore the state of their IT systems and capabilities. Appropriate board governance can go a long way toward helping a company avoid unnecessary risk and improve its competitive position.

FedEx, among others, have taken this step, creating board-level IT committees that are on a par with their audit, compensation, and governance committees. When the IT governance committee in one of these companies assists the CEO, the CIO, senior management, and the board in driving technology decisions, costly projects tend to remain under control, and the firm can carve out competitive advantage.

The question is no longer whether the board should be involved in IT decisions; the question is, how? Having observed the ever-changing IT strategies of hundreds of firms for over 40 years, we've found that there is no one-size-fits-all model for board supervision of a company's IT operations. The correct IT approach depends on a host of factors, including a company's history, industry, competitive situation, financial position, and quality of IT management. A strategy that works well for a clothing retailer is not appropriate for a large airline; the strategy that works for eBay can't work for a cement company. Creating a board-level committee is not, however, a best practice all companies should adopt. For many firms—consulting firms, small retailers, and book publishers, for instance—it would be a waste of time.

In this article, we show board members how to recognize their firms' positions and decide whether they should take a more aggressive stance. We illustrate the conditions under which boards should be less or more involved in IT decisions. We delineate what an IT governance committee should look like in terms of charter, membership, duties, and overall agenda. We offer recommendations for developing IT governance policies that take into account an organization's operational and strategic needs, as well as suggest what to do when those needs change. As we demonstrate in the following pages, appropriate board governance can go a long way toward helping a company avoid unnecessary risk and improve its competitive position.

The Four Modes

We've found it helpful to define the board's involvement according to two strategic issues: The first is how much the company relies on cost-effective, uninterrupted, secure, smoothly operating technology systems (what we refer to as "defensive" IT). The second is how much the company relies on IT for its competitive edge through systems that provide new value-added services and products or high responsiveness to customers ("offensive" IT). Depending on where companies locate themselves on a matrix we call "The IT Strategic Impact Grid" (see exhibit), technology governance may be a routine matter best handled by the existing audit committee or a vital asset that requires intense board-level scrutiny and assistance.

Defensive IT is about operational reliability. Keeping IT systems up and running is more important in the company's current incarnation than leapfrogging the competition through the clever use of emerging technology. One famously defensive firm is American Airlines, which developed the SABRE reservation system in the late 1960s. Once a source of innovation and strategic advantage, the SABRE system is now the absolute backbone of American's operations: When the system goes down, the airline grinds to a complete halt. Boards of firms like this need assurance that the technology systems are totally protected against

The IT strategic impact grid

How a board goes about governing IT activities generally depends on a company's size, industry, and competitive landscape. Companies in support mode are least dependent on IT; those in factory mode are much more dependent on it but are relatively unambitious when it comes to strategic use. Firms in turnaround mode expect that new systems will change their business; those in strategic mode require dependable systems as well as emerging technologies to hold or advance their competitive positions.

Defensive	Offensive
Factory mode	**Strategic mode**
✱ If systems fail for a minute or more, there's an immediate loss of business.	✱ If systems fail for a minute or more, there's an immediate loss of business.
✱ Decrease in response time beyond one second has serious consequences for both internal and external users.	✱ Decrease in response time beyond one second has serious consequences for both internal and external users.
✱ Most core business activities are online.	✱ New systems promise major process and service transformations.
✱ Systems work is mostly maintenance.	✱ New systems promise major cost reductions.
✱ Systems work provides little strategic differentiation or dramatic cost reduction.	✱ New systems will close significant cost, service, or process performance gap with competitors.
Support mode	**Turnaround mode**
✱ Even with repeated service interruptions of up to 12 hours, there are no serious consequences.	✱ New systems promise major process and service transformations.
✱ User response time can take up to five seconds with online transactions.	✱ New systems promise major cost reductions.
✱ Internal systems are almost invisible to suppliers and customers. There's little need for extranet capability.	✱ New systems will close significant cost, service, or process performance gap with competitors.
✱ Company can quickly revert to manual procedures for 80% of value transactions.	✱ IT constitutes more than 50% of capital spending.
✱ Systems work is mostly maintenance.	✱ IT makes up more than 15% of total corporate expenses.

Vertical axis: Low to high need for reliable information technology

Horizontal axis: Low to high need for new information technology

potential operational disasters—computer bugs, power interruptions, hacking, and so on—and that costs remain under control.

Offensive IT places strategic issues either over, or on the same level as, reliability. Offensive IT projects tend to be ambitious and risky because they often involve substantial organizational change. An offensive stance is called for when a company needs to alter its technology strategy to compete more effectively or to raise the firm to a position of industry leadership. Because of the resources required to take an offensive position, financially and competitively strong companies usually have to be intensively involved in IT on all levels. Wal-Mart, for example, is replacing bar codes with radio frequency identification (RFID) technology, which effectively drives the supply chain directly from the supplier to the warehouse without the need for scanning by associates.

Firms can be either defensive or offensive in their strategic approach to IT—approaches we call "modes." Let's look at each mode in turn.

Support Mode (Defensive)
Firms in this mode have both a relatively low need for reliability and a low need for strategic IT; technology fundamentally exists to support employees' activities. The Spanish clothier Zara, which began as a small retail shop, is a good example; the company keeps strict control over its supply chain operations by designing, producing, and distributing its own clothing. Though IT is used in these areas, the company won't suffer terribly if

a system goes down. (For more on Zara, see Kasra Ferdows, Michael A. Lewis, and Jose A.D. Machuca, "Rapid-Fire Fulfillment," HBR November 2004.) Core business systems are generally run on a batch cycle; most error correction and backup work is done manually. Customers and suppliers don't have access to internal systems. Companies in support mode can suffer repeated service interruptions of up to 12 hours without serious bottom-line consequences, and high-speed Internet response time isn't critical.

For such firms, the audit committee can review IT operations. The most critical questions for members to ask are: "Should we remain in support mode, or should we change our IT strategy to keep up with or surpass the competition?" and "Are we spending money wisely and not just chasing after new technology fads?" (In this mode, the spending mantra is, "Don't waste money." For a list of questions appropriate to each mode, see the exhibit "Asking the Tough Questions.")

Factory Mode (Defensive)

Companies in this mode need highly reliable systems but don't really require state-of-the-art computing. They resemble manufacturing plants; if the conveyor belts fail, production stops. (Airlines and other businesses that depend on fast, secure, real-time data response fall into this group.) These companies are much more dependent on the smooth operation of their technology, since most of their core business systems are online. They suffer an immediate loss of business if systems fail even for a minute; a reversion to manual

Asking the tough questions

What board members need to know about IT depends on the company's strategic position. Firms in support and factory mode should have their audit committees, with the help of an IT expert, query management. Organizations in turnaround and strategic mode will want the assistance of a full-fledged IT committee in getting answers to their questions.

*If your company is in **Support Mode,** ask the questions in set **A.***

*If your company is in **Factory Mode,** ask the questions in sets **A** and **B.***

*If your company is in **Turnaround Mode,** ask the questions in sets **A** and **C.***

*If your company is in **Strategic Mode,** ask the questions in sets **A, B,** and **C.***

A

- Has the strategic importance of our IT changed?
- What are our current and potential competitors doing in the area of IT?
- Are we following best practices in asset management?
- Is the company getting adequate ROI from information resources?
- Do we have the appropriate IT infrastructure and applications to exploit the development of our intellectual assets?

B

- Has anything changed in disaster recovery and security that will affect our business's continuity planning?
- Do we have in place management practices that will prevent our hardware, software, and legacy applications from becoming obsolete?
- Do we have adequate protection against denial of service attacks and hackers?
- Are there fast-response processes in place in the event of an attack?
- Do we have management processes in place to ensure 24/7 service levels, including tested backup?
- Are we protected against possible intellectual-property-infringement lawsuits?
- Are there any possible IT-based surprises lurking out there?

C

- Are our strategic IT development plans proceeding as required?
- Is our applications portfolio sufficient to deal with a competitive threat or to meet a potential opportunity?
- Do we have processes in place that will enable us to discover and execute any strategic IT opportunities?
- Do we have processes in place to guard against IT risk?
- Do we regularly benchmark to maintain our competitive cost structure?

procedures is difficult, if not impossible. Factory-mode firms generally depend on their extranets to communicate with customers and suppliers. Typically, factory-mode organizations are not interested in being the first to implement a new technology, but their top management and boards need to be aware of leading-edge practice and monitor the competitive landscape for any change that would require a more aggressive use of IT.

Because business continuity in IT operations is critical for these firms, the board needs to make sure that disaster recovery and security procedures are in place. The audit committee for a large East Coast medical center, for example, recently authorized a full disaster recovery, security, and operational environment review simply to ensure that appropriate safeguards were there. The study was expensive but completely necessary because, in the event of a failure, patients' lives would be at risk. (In this mode, the spending mantra is, "Don't cut corners.")

Turnaround Mode (Offensive)
Companies in the midst of strategic transformation frequently bet the farm on new technology. In this mode, technology typically accounts for more than 50% of capital expenditures and more than 15% of corporate costs. New systems promise major process and service improvements, cost reductions, and a competitive edge. At the same time, companies in this mode have a comparatively low need for reliability when it comes to existing business systems; like companies in support mode, they can withstand repeated service interruptions of up to

12 hours without serious consequences, and core business activities remain on a batch cycle. Once the new systems are installed, however, there is no possible reversion to manual systems because all procedures have been captured into databases.

Companies usually enter turnaround mode with a major IT project that requires a big reengineering effort, often accompanied by the decision to outsource or move a substantial portion of their operations offshore. Most firms don't spend a long time in turnaround mode; once the change is made, they move into either factory mode or strategic mode. American Airlines functioned in turnaround mode when it created the SABRE system; now it lives in factory mode. Similarly, the Canadian company St. Marys Cement operated in support mode until it began equipping its trucks with GPS devices, which pushed it into temporary turnaround mode.

Board oversight is critical for companies in turnaround mode; strategic IT plans must proceed on schedule and on budget, particularly when competitive advantage is at stake. (Here, the spending mantra is, "Don't screw it up.")

Strategic Mode (Offensive)

For some companies, total innovation is the name of the game. New technology informs not only the way they approach the marketplace but also the way they carry out daily operations. Strategic-mode firms need as much reliability as factory-mode firms do, but they also aggressively pursue process and service opportunities, cost reductions, and competitive advantages. Like turn-around firms, their IT expenditures are large.

Not every firm wants or needs to be in this mode; some are forced into it by competitive pressures. Consider Boeing, a company that dominated the commercial-airline-manufacturing industry until Airbus took the lead. Now convinced that its future rests on the successful design, marketing, and delivery of a new commercial plane, Boeing has embarked on an ambitious technology project that it hopes will return the company to industry dominance. Its new 787 plane, due in 2008, will be equipped with a new lightweight carbon composite skin. Since carbon composite skin is a relatively new material to be used so extensively in a commercial airplane, a neural network will be embedded in the fuselage and wings to constantly monitor load factors and make adjustments as changing conditions warrant. The 787 will be manufactured and assembled through the world's largest project management system, which will simultaneously coordinate thousands of computers and automate an integrated supply chain comprising hundreds of global partners. Each supplier will send components via specially equipped 747s to Boeing's site in Everett, Washington, where the 787 will be assembled in a mere three days, ensuring low costs and fast delivery. The 787 is like a jig-saw puzzle whose pieces must fall into perfect alignment at once, making Boeing both operationally and strategically dependent on IT.

As is the case for firms in turnaround mode, board-level IT governance is critical in strategic mode. Organizations require a fully formed IT oversight committee with at least one IT expert as a member. (The mantra for strategic-mode companies is, "Spend what it takes, and monitor results like crazy.")

As we said at the outset, the specific action a company should take with respect to IT oversight depends on which mode it's in. Regardless of its business, it behooves any company to take an in-depth look at its current business through the IT lens. In doing so, a company gains a much firmer grasp of what it needs to be successful.

How to Conduct IT Oversight

Having identified which mode they currently inhabit, companies then need to decide what kind of IT expertise they need on the board. Firms that require a high level of reliability need to focus on managing IT risk. The job of these boards is to assure the completeness, quality, security, reliability, and maintenance of existing IT investments that support day-to-day business processes. Rarely will such companies want a separate IT committee. Instead, the audit committee must do double duty as the IT governance team and delve deeply into the quality of the company's IT systems.

On the other hand, companies that need to go beyond defensive mode require an independent IT governance committee, rather than just having an IT expert serve on the audit committee. The IT governance committee's job is to keep the board apprised of what other organizations—particularly competitors—are doing with technology. Below, we outline the general duties of boards according to their modes.

Inventory the assets (all modes)

A board needs to understand the overall architecture of its company's IT applications portfolio as well as its asset management strategy. The first step is to find out what kinds of hardware, software, and information the company owns so as to determine whether it's getting adequate return from its IT investments.

Physical IT assets—counted as computer hardware—are relatively easy to inventory; intangible assets are not. Despite the fact that intangible assets have largely been ignored by the accounting field, most companies are increasingly reliant on them. Companies have huge investments in applications software, ranging from customer and HR databases to integrated supply chains. The board must ensure that management knows what information resources are out there, what condition they are in, and what role they play in generating revenue. One rule of thumb in determining intangible assets is to first measure the hardware inventory—including all mainframes, servers, and PCs—and then multiply that by ten. This renders a rough notion of what the software inventory will be (including off-the-shelf and proprietary software). The next step is to assure that the IT organization sorts the wheat from the chaff by determining the number and location of aging and legacy programs, and then decide which should be upgraded or maintained.

The board will also want to ensure that its company has the right IT infrastructure and applications in place to develop intellectual assets such as customer feedback about products and services. It needs to know how well employees can use IT systems to analyze customer feedback and develop or improve products and services.

Assure security and reliability (factory and strategic modes)

Ideally, boards of companies in factory and strategic modes should conduct regular reviews of their security and reliability measures so that any interruption of service doesn't send a company into a tailspin. Unfortunately, and all too often, oversight takes place following a crisis.

With the development of highly integrated IT networks within and outside the company, proper security has become paramount. An attack by a hacker or a virus can reduce profits by millions of dollars. An attack on Amazon, for example, would cost the company $600,000 an hour in revenue. If Cisco's systems were down for a day, the company would lose $70 million in revenues. Thus, the board needs to ensure that management is continually evaluating the company's networks for security breaches. (Some companies actually work with would-be hackers to test vulnerability to threats.)

A board will also want to make sure that service outages don't occur in the case of power failures or natural disasters. IT services are analogous to electrical power; an outage of days can trigger the demise of a company, particularly one in defensive mode. For this reason, backup systems must be continually tested to make sure that they actually work. IT also needs to ensure that service continues even while maintenance is under way, so proper detours and backups need to be in place. Many companies use diesel generators to keep backup systems running, but as the gigantic power outage that struck the East Coast of the U.S. in August 2003 demonstrated, the diesel can run out if the backup systems are in continuous use. In such cases, companies must take special steps. (Following the 2003 blackout, Delta Air Lines arranged for generator fuel to arrive by helicopter in the event of another shortage.)

Avoid surprises (factory, turnaround, and strategic modes)

No board wants to be taken unawares, and the most frequent source of IT-related surprises is from lax or ineffective project management. The larger the IT project, the higher the risk. Consider what happened to candy maker Hershey's when an expansion of its brand new ERP system blew up in the company's face. By the time Halloween rolled around, the company still could not keep track of orders, revenues, and inventory. Best estimates are that this cost the company $151 million.

Even companies that are supposed to be technology experts can botch a project, as EDS proved when it lost $2 billion on a contract to build an intranet for the U.S. Navy. Because EDS didn't fully understand the scope of the strategically important Navy initiative, the project suffered from unexpected delays and technical setbacks, costing EDS massive write-downs that ultimately drove its debt to junk bond status. To avoid such unwanted surprises, boards must ensure that appropriate project management systems are in place and that key decision points along the way are elevated to the appropriate level so that management can decide whether the project is still worth doing.

Companies can also be caught unawares if they don't have adequate service level agreements (SLAs) with vendors or clients, particularly when they choose to outsource their IT activities. A solid, well-thought-out SLA that makes explicit specific terms, deliverables, and responsibilities can help firms avoid serious project management problems. The agreement should guarantee that the needs of all the diverse groups within the company—such as marketing, sales, call center operations, and bad debt collection—are met under the terms of the agreement.

Additionally, legacy systems can present unwanted surprises because companies are so dependent on them, as the Y2K problem demonstrated. Rather than replace those systems, companies tend to build on top of them. And firms running batch-oriented systems often overlay them with new online user interfaces. This can create serious problems for accounting departments: A user of an online query system, for example, may believe that the answer he or she receives is up-to-the-minute; but if, in fact, data files are updated in batch mode, the information could be many hours out of date. Having to sort through such misinformation might require accounting departments to hire additional staff to ensure that financial reporting is done on time. To avoid such problems, the governance committee needs to decide whether it is more economical to maintain legacy hardware, software, and applications or to replace them. It's relatively easy for IT departments to determine when computer hardware needs upgrading. But when it comes to intangible assets such as legacy databases, the question of maintenance versus replacement becomes trickier; it's not uncommon to find maintenance taking up 90% of IT programming expenditures.

Watch out for legal problems (turnaround and strategic modes)

Companies can be subject to legal problems if they don't tread carefully around the intellectual property issues relating to IT. The advent of the Linux operating system, for example, has been a boon to many companies; at the same time, making free use of associated patented intellectual property has exposed them to legal risks. Consider SCO's $3 billion lawsuit against IBM, in which SCO alleges that IBM illegally incorporated SCO's intellectual property to the code base of the Linux operating system. Cases like this have made it clear that organizations need to stay alert for possible problems and avoid the expensive distraction of an intellectual property dispute involving IT. The board needs to watch out for such risks and be ready to bring in appropriate legal counsel when necessary to keep the senior management team from being distracted.

Keep an eye out for fresh threats and opportunities (turnaround and strategic modes)

It's a good idea for committee members to interrogate the CIO and line management about new products they may have seen or heard about at technology trade shows or industry conferences. It is also good practice to monitor firms in other industries that have a reputation for making effective use of leading-edge technology applications.

The committee must be on the lookout for technology-based competitive threats that could place a company in what we call "strategic jeopardy," which occurs when executive management is asleep at the switch vis-à-vis the competition. For example, the board can hire, or ask management to hire, a consulting company to gather intelligence, do benchmarking, and develop a scenario of possible threats from competitors, as well as outline opportunities. IT committees should also be sure that management has created a good customer feedback system that allows customers to offer opinions about competitors' products and services. In addition, it's important to monitor companies that may have the means and inclination to become competitors. Had supermarket chains been apprised of what Wal-Mart was up to with RFID, they might not have found themselves blindsided by the retail giant's aggressive supply-chain advances in the grocery business.

Finally, boards of firms in offensive modes must constantly scan for opportunities as technologies advance and the cost of computing drops. Anything that has been performed manually, for example, presents an opportunity not only to automate but also to raise the bar for products or services. Otis Elevator, for instance, dramatically improved its product delivery cycle by intelligently using IT to replace a paper-based tracking and fulfillment system. Once a contract for an elevator, escalator, or walkway is signed, a program called eLogistics sends project information directly from the field via nearly 1,000 local area networks and 1,000 global wide-area networks to contract logistics centers. The result has been a huge drop in inventory and a fivefold improvement in delivery time.

Building the IT Governance Committee

How do you set up an IT governance committee? A company that decides it needs board-level IT oversight must do three things: select the appropriate members and the chairman, determine the group's relationship to the audit committee, and prepare the charter. The first two are especially important.

We recommend that the IT governance group be made up of independent directors, as is the case with audit and compensation committees. Chairmanship is also critical. For firms in support, factory, or turnaround modes, the chairperson need not be an IT expert but should certainly be a tough-minded, IT-savvy business executive—either a CEO or a top manager who has overseen the use of IT to gain strategic advantage in another organization.

In any case, at least one person on the committee should be an IT expert who should operate as a peer at the senior management and board level. The expert's job is to challenge entrenched in-house thinking. He or she should not think ill of technology-averse cultures and must be a skilled communicator who does not hide behind technology jargon or talk down to board members. The expert should help the committee avoid dwelling on the difficulties of the work and emphasize instead the opportunities. The focus should be on the big picture: Conversations about IT strategy are hard and can be discouraging if the committee gets dragged down in technical details. (In fact, when looking for someone who fits these criteria, boards may find that many talented CIOs and CTOs drop off the list of potential IT committee members.) The IT expert must have not only a solid grounding in the firm's overall business needs but also a holistic view of the organization and its systems architecture. This is particularly important if the firm chooses to outsource its functions and connect multiple vendors across a network. The expert must also thoroughly understand the underlying dynamics governing changes in technology and their potential to alter the business's economic outlook.

Generally speaking, the IT expert serves much the same function as the certified financial expert on an audit committee. A CIO or CTO with solid experience in the management of IT qualifies; for example, the IT oversight committee chairman for the Great Atlantic & Pacific Tea Company (A&P) was previously CEO of an extremely successful supermarket chain on the West Coast, where he achieved impressive business results through effective IT system implementation and management. As chair of the IT committee, he helps balance his company's short-term business needs with long-term IT investments.

Unfortunately, skilled, business-oriented technology strategists are in short supply. In the absence of such a person within a company, an IT consultant who can help sort out technology issues can fit the bill, as might a divisional CEO or COO who is actively managing IT. Alternatively, a manager who has served in an influential technology company such as Microsoft or Oracle can help a firm determine its place on the strategic impact grid, begin to embrace emerging technologies, and locate other experts who can serve on the committee.

Businesses in strategic mode should have an IT oversight committee chaired by an IT expert. In this mode, it's even more important to get the membership right. For example, the chairman of the IT committee for Novell—a company in strategic mode—founded a major IT-strategy-consulting company, sold it to one of the then Big Six accounting firms, and continued as a senior partner in that firm's IT consulting business. Two other members of Novell's IT committee previously served as CIOs in major *Fortune* 100 companies; they also serve on Novell's audit committee.

We recommend that the relationship of the IT governance committee to the audit committee be very close, because IT issues can affect economic and regulatory matters such as Sarbanes-Oxley compliance. For this reason, it's a good idea to have one audit committee member serve on the IT oversight committee. The charter of the IT committee should explicitly describe its relationship to

An IT governance committee calendar

To be successful, an IT oversight committee must ensure that its discussions with senior management are deep and ongoing. The committee can help management visualize FT's impact on the firm. We recommend that it develop a to-do calendar of the defensive, offensive, and administrative oversight tasks it needs to carry out over the year. Here's a sample calendar.

Defensive governance	Frequency
IT projects/architecture	
Receive update of strategic projects.	Quarterly
Receive update of technical architecture and critique it.	As needed
Ensure update of applications architecture and critique it.	As needed
Receive and review update of project investments.	Annual
IT security	
Critique IT security practices.	Annual
Review and appraise IT disaster-recovery capabilities.	Annual
Review security-related audit findings.	As needed
Review current developments in security practices, standards, and new security-related technology strategies.	Annual
Internal controls	
Review IT internal control practices.	Annual
Review IT-related audit findings.	As needed
Send reports to audit committee regarding IT systems and processes affecting internal controls.	Annual

Offensive governance	Frequency
Advisory role	
Advise senior IT management team.	As needed
Stay informed of, assess, and advise the company's senior IT management team about new technologies, applications, and systems that relate to or affect the company's IT strategy or programs.	As needed
Receive update of IT strategy and critique it.	Annual
Review and critique business plan (annual and three-year).	Annual

(Continued)

(Continued)

Review internal IT assessment measurements and critique action plan.	Annual
Hold private session with CFO.	Quarterly

Strategic technology scanning

Visit other companies to observe technology approaches and strategies.	Annual
Engage outside experts as required to provide third-party opinions about company's technology strategy.	As needed
Report to the board on matters within the scope of the committee, as well as on any special issues that merit the board's attention.	Quarterly
Perform other duties as appropriate to ensure that the company's IT programs effectively support the company's business objectives and strategies.	As needed

Administrative	**Frequency**
Review and assess the adequacy of the IT oversight charter and recommend proposed changes to the board.	As needed
Evaluate IT oversight committee's effectiveness (self-assessment).	Annual
Approve minutes of prior meetings.	Quarterly
Present report to board regarding the IT oversight committee's activities.	Annual
Hold executive session with committee members.	As needed
Approve IT committee meeting planner for the upcoming year, and approve mutual expectations with management.	Annual

---

the audit group, as well as its organization, purpose, oversight responsibilities, and meeting schedule (see the exhibit "An IT Governance Committee Calendar").

Regardless of a company's position, top-level commitment is critical if the board is to engage in IT governance. Board members and senior managers must identify and carefully gauge their current positions on the IT impact grid and decide whether setting up an IT oversight committee is necessary, given the company's current situation. If the need is not clearly understood, or if general buy-in for establishing such a committee—which necessarily includes an IT expert among its members—doesn't exist, then the company shouldn't do it. Any effort to do so will be a waste of time, and failure will sour the chances of establishing such a committee later.

That said, it's clear that as more and more companies in support and factory modes change tactics, and as other firms choose to adopt new technologies to stay ahead of the game, board-level technology governance will become increasingly important. This is good news, for when top managers understand the degree to which they must be accountable for technology, for project expenditures, and for monitoring return on investment from IT, they will do a better job of ensuring that critical systems function as promised. One thing is certain: Given the dizzying pace of change in the world of technology, and the changes IT can force upon a business, there is no such thing as too much accountability.

RICHARD NOLAN is a professor of management and organization at the University of Washington in Seattle. **F. WARREN MCFARLAN** is the Albert H. Gordon Professor of Business Administration, Emeritus, at Harvard Business School.

Originally published in October 2005. Reprint R0510F

Competing on Analytics

by Thomas H. Davenport

WE ALL KNOW THE POWER OF THE KILLER APP. Over the years, groundbreaking systems from companies such as American Airlines (electronic reservations), Otis Elevator (predictive maintenance), and American Hospital Supply (online ordering) have dramatically boosted their creators' revenues and reputations. These heralded— and coveted—applications amassed and applied data in ways that upended customer expectations and optimized operations to unprecedented degrees. They transformed technology from a supporting tool into a strategic weapon.

Companies questing for killer apps generally focus all their firepower on the one area that promises to create the greatest competitive advantage. But a new breed of company is upping the stakes. Organizations such as Amazon, Harrah's, Capital One, and the Boston Red Sox have dominated their fields by deploying industrial-strength analytics across a wide variety of activities. In essence, they are transforming their organizations into armies of killer apps and crunching their way to victory.

Organizations are competing on analytics not just because they can—business today is awash in data and data crunchers—but also because they should. At a time when firms in many industries offer similar products and use comparable technologies, business processes are among the last remaining points of differentiation. And analytics competitors wring every last drop of value from those processes. So, like other companies, they know what products their customers want, but they also know what prices those customers will pay, how many items each will buy in a lifetime, and what triggers will make people buy more. Like other companies, they know compensation costs and turnover rates, but they can also calculate how much personnel contribute to or detract from the bottom line and how salary levels relate to individuals' performance. Like other companies, they know when inventories are running low, but they can also predict problems with demand and supply chains, to achieve low rates of inventory and high rates of perfect orders.

And analytics competitors do all those things in a coordinated way, as part of an overarching strategy championed by top leadership and pushed down to decision makers at every level. Employees hired for their expertise with numbers or trained to recognize their importance are armed with the best evidence and the best quantitative tools. As a result, they make the best decisions: big and small, every day, over and over and over.

Idea in Brief

It's virtually impossible to differentiate yourself from competitors based on products alone. Your rivals sell offerings similar to yours. And thanks to cheap offshore labor, you're hard-pressed to beat overseas competitors on product cost.

How to pull ahead of the pack? Become an **analytics competitor:** Use sophisticated data-collection technology and analysis to wring every last drop of value from all your business processes. With analytics, you discern not only what your customers want but also how much they're willing to pay and what keeps them loyal. You look beyond compensation costs to calculate your workforce's exact contribution to your bottom line. And you don't just track existing inventories; you also predict and prevent future inventory problems.

Analytics competitors seize the lead in their fields. Capital One's analytics initiative, for example, has spurred at least 20% growth in earnings per share every year since the company went public.

Make analytics part of *your* overarching competitive strategy, and push it down to decision makers at every level. You'll arm your employees with the best evidence and quantitative tools for making the best decisions—big and small, every day.

Although numerous organizations are embracing analytics, only a handful have achieved this level of proficiency. But analytics competitors are the leaders in their varied fields—consumer products, finance, retail, and travel and entertainment among them. Analytics has been instrumental to Capital One, which has exceeded 20% growth in earnings per share every year since it became a public company. It has allowed Amazon to dominate online retailing and turn a profit despite enormous investments in growth and infrastructure. In sports, the real secret weapon isn't steroids, but stats, as dramatic

Idea in Practice

To become an analytics competitor:

Champion Analytics from the Top. Acknowledge and endorse the changes in culture, processes, and skills that analytics competition will mean for much of your workforce. And prepare yourself to lead an analytics-focused organization: You will have to understand the theory behind various quantitative methods so you can recognize their limitations. If you lack background in statistical methods, consult experts who understand your business and know how analytics can be applied to it.

Create a Single Analytics Initiative. Place all data-collection and analysis activities under a common leadership, with common technology and tools. You'll facilitate data sharing

and avoid the impediments of inconsistent reporting formats, data definitions, and standards.

Example: Procter & Gamble created a centrally managed "überanalytics" group of 100 analysts drawn from many different functions. It applies this critical mass of expertise to pressing cross-functional issues. For instance, sales and marketing analysts supply data on growth opportunities in existing markets to supply-chain analysts, who can then design more responsive supply networks.

Focus Your Analytics Effort. Channel your resources into analytics initiatives that most directly serve your overarching competitive strategy. Harrah's, for instance, aims much of its

victories by the Boston Red Sox, the New England Patriots, and the Oakland A's attest.

At such organizations, virtuosity with data is often part of the brand. Progressive makes advertising hay from its detailed parsing of individual insurance rates. Amazon customers can watch the company learning about them as its service grows more targeted with frequent purchases. Thanks to Michael Lewis's bestselling book *Moneyball,* which demonstrated the power

analytical activity at improving customer loyalty, customer service, and related areas such as pricing and promotions.

Establish an Analytics Culture. Instill a companywide respect for measuring, testing, and evaluating quantitative evidence. Urge employees to base decisions on hard facts. Gauge and reward performance the same way—applying metrics to compensation and rewards.

Hire the Right People. Pursue and hire analysts who possess top-notch quantitative-analysis skills, can express complex ideas in simple terms, and can interact productively with decision makers. This combination may be difficult to find, so start recruiting well before you need to fill analyst positions.

Use the Right Technology. Prepare to spend significant resources on technology such as customer relationship management (CRM) or enterprise resource planning (ERP) systems. Present data in standard formats, integrate it, store it in a data warehouse, and make it easily accessible to everyone. And expect to spend years gathering enough data to conduct meaningful analyses.

Example: It took Dell Computer seven years to create a database that includes 1.5 million records of all its print, radio, broadcast TV, and cable ads. Dell couples the database with data on sales for each region in which the ads appeared (before and after their appearance). The information enables Dell to fine-tune its promotions for every medium—in every region.

of statistics in professional baseball, the Oakland A's are almost as famous for their geeky number crunching as they are for their athletic prowess.

To identify characteristics shared by analytics competitors, I and two of my colleagues at Babson College's Working Knowledge Research Center studied 32 organizations that have made a commitment to quantitative, fact-based analysis. Eleven of those organizations we classified as full-bore analytics competitors, meaning top management had announced that analytics was key to their strategies; they had multiple initiatives under way involving complex data and statistical analysis, and they managed analytical activity at the enterprise (not departmental) level.

This article lays out the characteristics and practices of these statistical masters and describes some of the very substantial changes other companies must undergo in order to compete on quantitative turf. As one would expect, the transformation requires a significant investment in technology, the accumulation of massive stores of data, and the formulation of companywide strategies for managing the data. But at least as important, it requires executives' vocal, unswerving commitment and willingness to change the way employees think, work, and are treated. As Gary Loveman, CEO of analytics competitor Harrah's, frequently puts it, "Do we think this is true? Or do we know?"

Anatomy of an Analytics Competitor

One analytics competitor that's at the top of its game is Marriott International. Over the past 20 years, the corporation has honed to a science its system for establishing the optimal price for guest rooms (the key analytics process in hotels, known as revenue management). Today, its ambitions are far grander. Through its Total Hotel Optimization program, Marriott has expanded its quantitative expertise to areas such as conference facilities and catering, and made related tools available over the Internet to property revenue managers and hotel owners. It has developed systems to optimize offerings to frequent customers and assess the likelihood of those customers' defecting to competitors. It has given local revenue managers the power to override the system's recommendations when certain local factors can't be predicted (like the large number of Hurricane Katrina evacuees arriving in Houston). The company has even created a revenue opportunity model, which computes actual revenues as a percentage of the optimal rates that could have been charged. That figure has grown from 83% to 91% as Marriott's revenue-management analytics has taken root throughout the enterprise. The word is out among property owners and franchisees: If you want to squeeze the most revenue from your inventory, Marriott's approach is the ticket.

Clearly, organizations such as Marriott don't behave like traditional companies. Customers notice the difference in every interaction; employees and vendors live the difference every day. Our study found three key attributes among analytics competitors:

Widespread use of modeling and optimization

Any company can generate simple descriptive statistics about aspects of its business—average revenue per employee, for example, or average order size. But analytics competitors look well beyond basic statistics. These companies use predictive modeling to identify the most profitable customers—plus those with the greatest profit potential and the ones most likely to cancel their accounts. They pool data generated in-house and data acquired from outside sources (which they analyze more deeply than do their less statistically savvy competitors) for a comprehensive understanding of their customers. They optimize their supply chains and can thus determine the impact of an unexpected constraint, simulate alternatives, and route shipments around problems. They establish prices in real time to get the highest yield possible from each of their customer transactions. They create complex models of how their operational costs relate to their financial performance.

Leaders in analytics also use sophisticated experiments to measure the overall impact or "lift" of intervention strategies and then apply the results to continuously improve subsequent analyses. Capital One, for example, conducts more than 30,000 experiments a year, with different interest rates, incentives, direct-mail packaging, and other variables. Its goal is to maximize the likelihood both that potential customers will sign up for credit cards and that they will pay back Capital One.

Progressive employs similar experiments using widely available insurance industry data. The company defines narrow groups, or cells, of customers: for example, motorcycle riders ages 30 and above, with college educations, credit scores over a certain level, and no accidents. For each cell, the company performs a regression analysis to identify factors that most closely correlate with the losses that group engenders. It then sets prices for the cells, which should enable the company to earn a profit across a portfolio of customer groups, and uses simulation software to test the financial implications of those hypotheses. With this approach, Progressive can profitably insure customers in traditionally high-risk categories. Other insurers reject high-risk customers out of hand, without bothering to delve more deeply into the data (although even traditional competitors, such as Allstate, are starting to embrace analytics as a strategy).

An enterprise approach

Analytics competitors understand that most business functions—even those, like marketing, that have historically depended on art rather than science—can be improved with sophisticated quantitative techniques. These organizations don't gain advantage from one killer app, but rather from multiple applications supporting many parts of the business—and, in a few cases, being rolled out for use by customers and suppliers.

UPS embodies the evolution from targeted analytics user to comprehensive analytics competitor. Although the company is among the world's most rigorous practitioners of operations research and industrial engineering, its capabilities were, until fairly recently, narrowly focused. Today, UPS is wielding its statistical skill to track the movement of packages and to anticipate and influence the actions of people—assessing the likelihood of customer attrition and identifying sources of problems. The UPS Customer Intelligence Group, for example, is able to accurately predict customer defections by examining usage patterns and complaints. When the data point to a potential defector, a salesperson contacts that customer to review and resolve the problem, dramatically reducing the loss of accounts. UPS still lacks the breadth of initiatives of a full-bore analytics competitor, but it is heading in that direction.

Analytics competitors treat all such activities from all provenances as a single, coherent initiative, often massed under one rubric, such as "information-based strategy" at Capital One or "information-based customer management" at Barclays Bank. These programs operate not just under a common label but also under common leadership and with common technology and tools. In traditional companies, "business intelligence" (the term IT people use for analytics and reporting processes and software) is generally managed by departments; number-crunching functions select their own tools, control their own data warehouses, and train their own people. But that way, chaos lies. For one thing, the proliferation of user-developed spreadsheets and databases inevitably leads to multiple versions of key indicators within an organization. Furthermore, research has shown that between 20% and 40% of spreadsheets contain errors; the more spreadsheets floating around a company, therefore, the more fecund the breeding ground for mistakes. Analytics competitors, by contrast, field centralized groups to ensure that critical data and other resources are well managed and that different parts of the organization can share data easily, without the impediments of inconsistent formats, definitions, and standards.

Some analytics competitors apply the same enterprise approach to people as to technology. Procter & Gamble, for example, recently created a kind of überanalytics group consisting of more than 100 analysts from such functions as operations, supply chain, sales, consumer research, and marketing. Although most of the analysts are embedded in business operating units, the group is centrally managed. As a result of this consolidation, P&G can apply a critical mass of expertise to its most pressing issues. So, for example, sales and marketing analysts supply data on opportunities for growth in existing markets to analysts who design corporate supply networks. The supply chain analysts, in turn, apply their expertise in certain decision-analysis techniques to such new areas as competitive intelligence.

The group at P&G also raises the visibility of analytical and data-based decision making within the company. Previously, P&G's crack analysts had improved business processes and saved the firm money; but because they were squirreled away in dispersed domains, many executives didn't know what services they offered or how effective they could be. Now those executives are more likely to tap the company's deep pool of expertise for their projects. Meanwhile, masterful number crunching has become part of the story P&G tells to investors, the press, and the public.

Senior executive advocates

A companywide embrace of analytics impels changes in culture, processes, behavior, and skills for many employees. And so, like any major transition, it requires leadership from executives at the very top who have a passion for the quantitative approach. Ideally, the principal advocate is the CEO. Indeed, we found several chief executives who have driven the shift to analytics at their companies over the past few years, including Loveman of Harrah's, Jeff Bezos of Amazon, and Rich Fairbank of Capital One. Before he retired from the Sara Lee Bakery Group, former CEO Barry Beracha kept a sign on his desk that summed up his personal and organizational philosophy: "In God we trust. All others bring data." We did come across some companies in which a single functional or business unit leader was trying to push analytics throughout the organization, and a few were making some progress. But we found that these lower-level people lacked the clout, the perspective, and the cross-functional scope to change the culture in any meaningful way.

CEOs leading the analytics charge require both an appreciation of and a familiarity with the subject. A background in statistics isn't necessary, but those leaders must understand the theory behind various quantitative methods so that they recognize those methods' limitations—which factors are being weighed and which ones aren't. When the CEOs need help grasping quantitative techniques, they turn to experts who understand the business and how analytics can be applied to it. We interviewed several leaders who had retained such advisers, and these executives stressed the need to find someone who can explain things in plain language and be trusted not to spin the numbers. A few CEOs we spoke with had surrounded themselves with very analytical people—professors, consultants, MIT graduates, and the like. But that was a personal preference rather than a necessary practice.

Of course, not all decisions should be grounded in analytics—at least not wholly so. Personnel matters, in particular, are often well and appropriately informed by instinct and anecdote. More organizations are subjecting recruiting and hiring decisions to statistical analysis (see the sidebar "Going to Bat for Stats"). But research shows that human beings can make quick, surprisingly accurate assessments of personality and character based on simple observations. For analytics-minded leaders, then, the challenge boils down to knowing when to run with the numbers and when to run with their guts.

Their Sources of Strength

Analytics competitors are more than simple number-crunching factories. Certainly, they apply technology—with a mixture of brute force and finesse—to multiple business problems. But they also direct their energies toward finding the right focus, building the right culture, and hiring the right people to make optimal use of the data they constantly churn. In the end, people and strategy, as much as information technology, give such organizations strength.

The right focus

Although analytics competitors encourage universal fact-based decisions, they must choose where to direct resource-intensive efforts. Generally, they pick several functions or initiatives that together serve an overarching strategy. Harrah's, for example, has aimed much of

Going to Bat for Stats

THE ANALYSIS-VERSUS-INSTINCT DEBATE, a favorite of political commentators during the last two U.S. presidential elections, is raging in professional sports, thanks to several popular books and high-profile victories. For now, analysis seems to hold the lead.

Most notably, statistics are a major part of the selection and deployment of players. *Moneyball,* by Michael Lewis, focuses on the use of analytics in player selection for the Oakland A's—a team that wins on a shoestring. The New England Patriots, a team that devotes an enormous amount of attention to statistics, won three of the last four Super Bowls, and their payroll is currently ranked 24th in the league. The Boston Red Sox have embraced "sabermetrics" (the application of analysis to baseball), even going so far as to hire Bill James, the famous baseball statistician who popularized that term. Analytic HR strategies are taking hold in European soccer as well. One leading team, Italy's A.C. Milan, uses predictive models from its Milan Lab research center to prevent injuries by analyzing physiological, orthopedic, and psychological data from a variety of sources. A fast-rising English soccer team, the

its analytical activity at increasing customer loyalty, customer service, and related areas like pricing and promotions. UPS has broadened its focus from logistics to customers, in the interest of providing superior service. While such multipronged strategies define analytics competitors, executives we interviewed warned companies against becoming too diffuse in their initiatives or losing clear sight of the business purpose behind each.

Another consideration when allocating resources is how amenable certain functions are to deep analysis. There are at least seven common targets for analytical

Bolton Wanderers, is known for its manager's use of extensive data to evaluate players' performance.

Still, sports managers—like business leaders—are rarely fact-or-feeling purists. St. Louis Cardinals manager Tony La Russa, for example, brilliantly combines analytics with intuition to decide when to substitute a charged-up player in the batting lineup or whether to hire a spark-plug personality to improve morale. In his recent book, *Three Nights in August*, Buzz Bissinger describes that balance: "La Russa appreciated the information generated by computers. He studied the rows and the columns. But he also knew they could take you only so far in baseball, maybe even confuse you with a fog of overanalysis. As far as he knew, there was no way to quantify desire. And those numbers told him exactly what he needed to know when added to twenty-four years of managing experience."

That final sentence is the key. Whether scrutinizing someone's performance record or observing the expression flitting across an employee's face, leaders consult their own experience to understand the "evidence" in all its forms.

activity, and specific industries may present their own (see "Things You Can Count On"). Statistical models and algorithms that dangle the possibility of performance breakthroughs make some prospects especially tempting. Marketing, for example, has always been tough to quantify because it is rooted in psychology. But now consumer products companies can hone their market research using multiattribute utility theory—a tool for understanding and predicting consumer behaviors and decisions. Similarly, the advertising industry is adopting econometrics—statistical techniques for measuring the lift provided by different ads and promotions over time.

Things you can count on

Analytics competitors make expert use of statistics and modeling to improve a wide variety of functions:

Function	Description	Exemplars
Supply chain	Simulate and optimize supply chain flows; reduce inventory and stock-outs.	Dell, Wal-Mart, Amazon
Customer selection, loyalty, and service	Identify customers with the greatest profit potential; increase likelihood that they will want the product or service offering; retain their loyalty.	Harrah's, Capital One, Barclays
Pricing	Identify the price that will maximize yield, or profit.	Progressive, Marriott
Human capital	Select the best employees for particular tasks or, jobs at particular compensation levels.	New England Patriots, Oakland A's, Boston Red Sox
Product and service quality	Detect quality problems early and minimize them.	Honda, Intel
Financial performance	Better understand the drivers of financial performance and the effects of nonfinancial factors.	MCI, Verizon
Research and development	Improve quality, efficacy, and, where applicable, safety of products and services.	Novartis, Amazon, Yahoo

The most proficient analytics practitioners don't just measure their own navels—they also help customers and vendors measure theirs. Wal-Mart, for example, insists that suppliers use its Retail Link system to monitor product movement by store, to plan promotions and layouts within stores, and to reduce stock-outs. E.&J. Gallo provides distributors with data and analysis on retailers' costs and pricing so they can calculate the per-bottle profitability for each of Gallo's 95 wines. The distributors, in turn, use that information to help retailers optimize their mixes while persuading them to add shelf space for Gallo products. Procter & Gamble offers data and analysis to its retail customers, as part of a program called Joint Value Creation, and to its suppliers to help improve responsiveness and reduce costs. Hospital supplier Owens & Minor furnishes similar services, enabling customers and suppliers to access and analyze their buying and selling data, track ordering patterns in search of consolidation opportunities, and move off-contract purchases to group contracts that include products distributed by Owens & Minor and its competitors. For example, Owens & Minor might show a hospital chain's executives how much money they could save by consolidating purchases across multiple locations or help them see the trade-offs between increasing delivery frequency and carrying inventory.

The right culture

Culture is a soft concept; analytics is a hard discipline. Nonetheless, analytics competitors must instill a companywide respect for measuring, testing, and evaluating quantitative evidence. Employees are urged to base decisions on hard facts. And they know that their performance is gauged the same way. Human resource organizations within analytics competitors are rigorous about applying metrics to compensation and rewards. Harrah's, for example, has made a dramatic change from a rewards culture based on paternalism and tenure to one based on such meticulously collected performance measurements as financial and customer service results. Senior executives also set a consistent example with their own behavior, exhibiting a hunger for and confidence in fact and analysis. One exemplar of such leadership was Beracha of the Sara Lee Bakery Group, known to his employees as a "data dog" because he hounded them for data to support any assertion or hypothesis.

Not surprisingly, in an analytics culture, there's sometimes tension between innovative or entrepreneurial impulses and the requirement for evidence. Some companies place less emphasis on blue-sky development, in which designers or engineers chase after a gleam in someone's eye. In these organizations, R&D, like other functions, is rigorously metric-driven. At Yahoo, Progressive, and Capital One, process and product changes are tested on a small scale and implemented as they are validated. That approach, well established within various academic and business disciplines (including engineering, quality management, and psychology), can be applied to most corporate processes—even to not-so-obvious candidates, like human resources and customer service. HR, for example, might create profiles of managers' personality traits and leadership styles and then test those managers in different situations. It could then compare data on individuals' performance with data about personalities to determine what traits are most important to managing a project that is behind schedule, say, or helping a new group to assimilate.

There are, however, instances when a decision to change something or try something new must be made too quickly for extensive analysis, or when it's not possible to gather data beforehand. For example, even though Amazon's Jeff Bezos greatly prefers to rigorously quantify users' reactions before rolling out new features, he couldn't test the company's search-inside-the-book offering without applying it to a critical mass of books (120,000, to begin with). It was also expensive to develop, and that increased the risk. In this case, Bezos trusted his instincts and took a flier. And the feature did prove popular when introduced.

The right people

Analytical firms hire analytical people—and like all companies that compete on talent, they pursue the best. When Amazon needed a new head for its global supply chain, for example, it recruited Gang Yu, a professor of management science and software entrepreneur who is one of the world's leading authorities on optimization analytics. Amazon's business model requires the company to manage a constant flow of new products, suppliers, customers, and promotions, as well as deliver orders by promised dates. Since his arrival, Yu and his team have been designing and building sophisticated supply chain systems to optimize those processes. And while he tosses around phrases like "nonstationary stochastic processes," he's also good at explaining the new approaches to Amazon's executives in clear business terms.

Established analytics competitors such as Capital One employ squadrons of analysts to conduct quantitative experiments and, with the results in hand, design credit card and other financial offers. These efforts call for a specialized skill set, as you can see from this job description (typical for a Capital One analyst):

> High conceptual problem-solving and quantitative analytical aptitudes...Engineering, financial, consulting, and/or other analytical quantitative educational/work background. Ability to quickly learn how to use software applications. Experience with Excel models. Some graduate work preferred but not required (e.g., MBA). Some experience with project management methodology, process improvement tools (Lean, Six Sigma), or statistics preferred.

Other firms hire similar kinds of people, but analytics competitors have them in much greater numbers. Capital One is currently seeking three times as many analysts as operations people—hardly the common practice for a bank. "We are really a company of analysts," one executive there noted. "It's the primary job in this place."

Good analysts must also have the ability to express complex ideas in simple terms and have the relationship skills to interact well with decision makers. One consumer products company with a 30-person analytics group looks for what it calls "PhDs with personality"— people with expertise in math, statistics, and data analysis who can also speak the language of business and help market their work internally and sometimes externally. The head of a customer analytics group at Wachovia Bank describes the rapport with others his group seeks: "We are trying to build our people as part of the business team," he explains. "We want them sitting at the business table, participating in a discussion of what the key issues are, determining what information needs the businesspeople have, and recommending actions to the business partners. We want this [analytics group] to be not just a general utility, but rather an active and critical part of the business unit's success."

Of course, a combination of analytical, business, and relationship skills may be difficult to find. When the software company SAS (a sponsor of this research, along with Intel) knows it will need an expert in state-of-the-art business applications such as predictive modeling or recursive partitioning (a form of decision tree analysis applied to very complex data sets), it begins recruiting up to 18 months before it expects to fill the position.

In fact, analytical talent may be to the early 2000s what programming talent was to the late 1990s. Unfortunately, the U.S. and European labor markets aren't exactly teeming with analytically sophisticated job candidates. Some organizations cope by contracting work to countries such as India, home to many statistical experts. That strategy may succeed when offshore analysts work on stand-alone problems. But if an iterative discussion with business decision makers is required, the distance can become a major barrier.

The right technology

Competing on analytics means competing on technology. And while the most serious competitors investigate the latest statistical algorithms and decision science approaches, they also constantly monitor and push the IT frontier. The analytics group at one consumer products company went so far as to build its own supercomputer because it felt that commercially available models were inadequate for its demands. Such heroic feats usually aren't necessary, but serious analytics does require the following:

A data strategy. Companies have invested many millions of dollars in systems that snatch data from every conceivable source. Enterprise resource planning, customer relationship management, point-of-sale, and other systems ensure that no transaction or other significant exchange occurs without leaving a mark. But to compete on that information, companies must present it in standard formats, integrate it, store it in a data warehouse, and make it easily accessible to anyone and everyone. And they will need *a lot* of it. For example, a company may spend several years accumulating data on different marketing approaches before it has gathered enough to reliably analyze the effectiveness of an advertising campaign. Dell employed DDB Matrix, a unit of the advertising agency DDB Worldwide, to create (over a period of seven years) a database that includes 1.5 million records on all the computer maker's print, radio, network TV, and cable ads, coupled with data on Dell sales for each region in which the ads appeared (before and after their appearance). That information allows Dell to fine-tune its promotions for every medium in every region.

Business intelligence software. The term "business intelligence," which first popped up in the late 1980s, encompasses a wide array of processes and software used to collect, analyze, and disseminate data, all in the interests of better decision making. Business intelligence tools allow employees to extract, transform, and load (or ETL, as people in the industry would say) data for analysis and then make those analyses available in reports, alerts, and scorecards. The popularity of analytics competition is partly a response to the emergence of integrated packages of these tools.

Computing hardware. The volumes of data required for analytics applications may strain the capacity of low-end computers and servers. Many analytics competitors are converting their hardware to 64-bit processors that churn large amounts of data quickly.

The Long Road Ahead

Most companies in most industries have excellent reasons to pursue strategies shaped by analytics. Virtually all the organizations we identified as aggressive analytics competitors are clear leaders in their fields, and they attribute much of their success to the masterful exploitation of data. Rising global competition intensifies the need for this sort of proficiency. Western companies

You Know You Compete on Analytics When...

1. You apply sophisticated information systems and rigorous analysis not only to your core capability but also to a range of functions as varied as marketing and human resources.

2. Your senior executive team not only recognizes the importance of analytics capabilities but also makes their development and maintenance a primary focus.

3. You treat fact-based decision making not only as a best practice but also as a part of the culture that's constantly emphasized and communicated by senior executives.

4. You hire not only people with analytical skills but a lot of people with *the very best* analytical skills—and consider them a key to your success.

5. You not only employ analytics in almost every function and department but also consider it so strategically important that you manage it at the enterprise level.

6. You not only are expert at number crunching but also invent proprietary metrics for use in key business processes.

7. You not only use copious data and in-house analysis but also share them with customers and suppliers.

8. You not only avidly consume data but also seize every opportunity to generate information, creating a "test and learn" culture based on numerous small experiments.

9. You not only have committed to competing on analytics but also have been building your capabilities for several years.

10. You not only emphasize the importance of analytics internally but also make quantitative capabilities part of your company's story, to be shared in the annual report and in discussions with financial analysts.

unable to beat their Indian or Chinese competitors on product cost, for example, can seek the upper hand through optimized business processes.

Companies just now embracing such strategies, however, will find that they take several years to come to fruition. The organizations in our study described a long, sometimes arduous journey. The UK Consumer Cards and Loans business within Barclays Bank, for example, spent five years executing its plan to apply analytics to the marketing of credit cards and other financial products. The company had to make process changes in virtually every aspect of its consumer business: underwriting risk, setting credit limits, servicing accounts, controlling fraud, cross selling, and so on. On the technical side, it had to integrate data on 10 million Barclaycard customers, improve the quality of the data, and build systems to step up data collection and analysis. In addition, the company embarked on a long series of small tests to begin learning how to attract and retain the best customers at the lowest price. And it had to hire new people with top-drawer quantitative skills.

Much of the time—and corresponding expense—that any company takes to become an analytics competitor will be devoted to technological tasks: refining the systems that produce transaction data, making data available in warehouses, selecting and implementing analytic software, and assembling the hardware and communications environment. And because those who don't record history are doomed not to learn from it, companies that have collected little information—or the wrong kind—will need to amass a sufficient body of data to support reliable forecasting. "We've been collecting data for six or seven years, but it's only become usable in the last two or three, because we needed time and experience to validate conclusions based on the data," remarked a manager of customer data analytics at UPS.

And, of course, new analytics competitors will have to stock their personnel larders with fresh people. (When Gary Loveman became COO, and then CEO, of Harrah's, he brought in a group of statistical experts who could design and implement quantitatively based marketing campaigns and loyalty programs.) Existing employees, meanwhile, will require extensive training. They need to know what data are available and all the ways the information can be analyzed; and they must learn to recognize such peculiarities and shortcomings as missing data, duplication, and quality problems. An analytics-minded executive at Procter & Gamble suggested to me that firms should begin to keep managers in their jobs for longer periods because of the time required to master quantitative approaches to their businesses.

The German pathologist Rudolph Virchow famously called the task of science "to stake out the limits of the knowable." Analytics competitors pursue a similar goal, although the universe they seek to know is a more circumscribed one of customer behavior, product movement, employee performance, and financial reactions. Every day, advances in technology and techniques give companies a better and better handle on the critical minutiae of their operations.

The Oakland A's aren't the only ones playing money-ball. Companies of every stripe want to be part of the game.

THOMAS H. DAVENPORT is the President's Distinguished Professor of Information Technology and Management at Babson College in Massachusetts.

Originally published in January 2006. Reprint R0601H

Investing in the IT That Makes a Competitive Difference

by Andrew McAfee and Erik Brynjolfsson

IT'S NOT JUST YOU. It really *is* getting harder to outpace the other guys. Our recent research finds that since the middle of the 1990s, which marked the mainstream adoption of the internet and commercial enterprise software, competition within the U.S. economy has accelerated to unprecedented levels. There are a number of possible reasons for this quickening, including M&A activity, the opening up of global markets, and companies' continuing R&D efforts. However, we found that a central catalyst in this shift is the massive increase in the power of IT investments.

To better understand when and where IT confers competitive advantage in today's economy, we studied all publicly traded U.S. companies in all industries from the 1960s through 2005, looking at relevant performance indicators from each (including sales, earnings, profitability, and market capitalization) and found some striking patterns: Since the mid-1990s, a new competitive dynamic has emerged—greater gaps between the leaders and laggards in an industry, more concentrated and winner-take-all markets, and more churn among rivals in a sector. Strikingly, this pattern closely matches the turbulent "creative destruction" mode of capitalism that was first predicted over 60 years ago by economist Joseph Schumpeter. This accelerated competition has coincided with a sharp increase in the quantity and quality of IT investments, as more organizations have moved to bolster (or altogether replace) their existing operating models using the internet and enterprise software. Tellingly, the changes in competitive dynamics are most apparent in precisely those sectors that have spent the most on information technology, even when we controlled for other factors.

This pattern is a familiar one in markets for digitized products like computer software and music. Those industries have long been dominated by both a winner-take-all dynamic and high turbulence, as each group of dominant innovators is threatened by succeeding waves of innovation. Consider how quickly Google supplanted Yahoo, which supplanted AltaVista and others that created the search engine market from nothing. Or the relative speed with which new recording artists can dominate sales in a category.

Most industries have historically been fairly immune from this kind of Schumpeterian competition. However, our findings show that the internet and enterprise

Idea in Brief

It's not just you. It really *is* getting harder to outpace the other guys. Since the mid-1990s, competition in the U.S. economy has accelerated to unprecedented levels. The engine behind this hypercompetition: IT. Thanks to powerful tools like ERP and CRM, backed by cheap networks, companies are swiftly replicating business-process innovations throughout their organizations. The firm with the best processes (order fulfillment, field installation, job closing) wins, but not for long. Rivals are striking back with their own IT-based process innovations.

To gain—and keep—a competitive edge in this environment, McAfee and Brynjolfsson recommend a three-step strategy:

- **Deploy** a consistent technology platform, rather than stitching together a jumble of legacy systems.
- **Innovate** better ways of working.
- **Propagate** those process innovations widely throughout your company.

By taking these steps, elevator-systems maker Otis realized not only dramatically shorter sales-cycle times but higher revenues and operating profit.

IT are now accelerating competition within traditional industries in the broader U.S. economy. Why? Not because more *products* are becoming digital but because more *processes* are: Just as a digital photo or a web-search algorithm can be endlessly replicated quickly and accurately by copying the underlying bits, a company's unique business processes can now be propagated with much higher fidelity across the organization by embedding it in enterprise information technology. As a result, an innovator with a better way of doing things can scale up with unprecedented speed to dominate an industry. In response, a rival can roll out further process innovations throughout its product

Idea in Practice

The authors recommend these steps for staying ahead of rivals through IT-enabled process innovation:

Deploy. Adopt a uniform technology platform to be used throughout your company.

> *Example:* Before deploying a consistent platform, Cisco's various units had nine different tools for checking an order's status. Each pulled information from different repositories and defined key terms differently, leading to circulation of conflicting order-status reports around the company. The company reconfigured its IT systems for consistent execution of key business processes including market to sell, lead to order, quote to cash, issue to resolution, forecast to build, idea to product, and hire to retire. The payoff?

Strong performance over the past few years.

Innovate. Design better ways of doing work in your company. The best candidates for innovation are processes that:

- Apply across a large swatch of your company (such as all your stores, factories, or delivery teams)

- Produce results as soon as your new IT system goes live

- Require precise instructions (such as order taking or delivery)

- Can be executed the same way everywhere and every time in your organization

- Can be tracked in real time so you can immediately spot and address any backsliding to older versions of the process

lines and geographic markets to recapture market share. Winners can win big and fast, but not necessarily for very long.

CVS, Cisco, and Otis Elevator are among the many companies we've observed gaining a market edge by competing on technology-enabled processes—carefully examining their working methods, revamping them in interesting ways, and using readily available enterprise

Example: U.K. grocery chain Tesco has long used customer-rewards cards to collect detailed data on individual purchases, to categorize customers, and to tailor offers. But it went one step further: tracking redemption rates for direct-marketing initiatives and tweaking its processes to get better responses from customers. Its process innovation drove its re-demption rate to 20%—far above the industry's average of 2%.

Propagate. Use IT to replicate process innovations through-out your company.

Example: At CVS pharma-cies, customer satisfaction was declining. The reason: Prescription orders were delayed during the insur-ance check, which was performed after customers had left the store. So cus-tomers weren't immedi-ately available to answer common questions such as "Have you changed jobs?" The company decided to move the insurance check forward in the prescription-fulfillment process, before the drug-safety review, so customers would still be around to answer questions.

The process change was embedded in the informa-tion systems that supported operations at all 4,000 CVS pharmacies in the United States. Performance improved across all the pharmacies, and customer satisfaction scores rose from 86% to 91%—a dramatic difference in the aggressive pharmacy market.

software and networking technologies to spread these process changes to far-flung locations so they're exe-cuted the same way every time.

In the following pages, we'll explore why the link between technology and competition has become much stronger and tighter since the mid-1990s, and we'll clarify the roles that business leaders and enterprise technologies should play in this new environment.

Competing at such high speeds isn't easy, and not everyone will be able to keep up. The senior executives who do may realize not only greatly improved business processes but also higher market share and increased market value.

How Technology Has Changed Competition

The mid-1990s marked a clear discontinuity in competitive dynamics and the start of a period of innovation in corporate IT, when the internet and enterprise software applications—like enterprise resource planning (ERP), customer relationship management (CRM), and enterprise content management (ECM)—became practical tools for business. Corporate investments in IT surged during this time—from about $3,500 spent per worker in 1994 to about $8,000 in 2005, according the U.S. Bureau of Economic Analysis (BEA). (See the exhibit "The IT Surge.") At the same time, annual productivity growth in U.S. companies roughly doubled, after plodding along at about 1.4% for nearly 20 years. Much attention has been paid to the connection between productivity growth and the increase in IT investment. But hardly any has been directed to the nature of the link between IT and competitiveness. That's why, with help from Harvard Business School researcher Michael Sorell and Feng Zhu, who's now an assistant professor at USC, we set out two years ago to compare the increase in IT spending with various measures of competition, focusing on three quantifiable indicators: concentration, turbulence, and performance spread.

The IT surge

The total real stock of IT hardware and software in the United States began to rise dramatically in the mid-1990s.

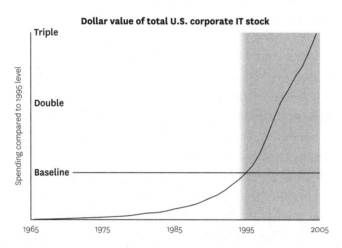

Dollar value of total U.S. corporate IT stock

Source: U.S. Bureau of Economic Analysis

In a *concentrated* or winner-take-all industry, just a few companies account for the bulk of the market share. For our study, we focused on the degree to which each industry became more or less concentrated over time. A sector is *turbulent* if the sales leaders in it are frequently leapfrogging one another in rank order. And finally the *performance spread* in an industry is large when the leaders and laggards differ greatly on standard performance measures such as return on assets, profit margins, and market capitalization per dollar of revenue—the kinds of numbers that matter a lot to senior managers and investors.

Were there economywide changes in these three measures after the mid-1990s, when IT spending accelerated? If so, were the changes more pronounced in industries that were more IT intensive—that is, where IT made up a larger share of all fixed assets within an industry? In a word, yes.

We analyzed industry data from the BEA, as well as from annual company reports, and found that average turbulence within U.S. industries rose sharply starting in the mid-1990s. Furthermore, after declining in previous decades, industry concentration reversed course and began increasing around the same time. Finally, the spread between the highest and lowest performers also increased. These changes coincided with the surge in IT investment and the concurrent productivity rise, suggesting a fundamental change in the underlying economics of competition. (See the exhibit "Competitive Dynamics: Several Ways to Slice IT.")

Looking more closely at the data, we found that the changes in dynamics were indeed greatest in those industries that were more IT intensive—for instance, consumer electronics and auto parts manufacturers. Further, we considered the role of M&A activity, globalization, and R&D spending in our analysis of the competitive landscape and found some minor correlations—but none strong enough to override our measures (see the sidebar "Is IT the Only Factor That Matters?").

One interpretation of our findings might be that IT is, indeed, inducing the intensified competition we've documented—but that the change in dynamics is only temporary. According to this argument, the years since

Competitive dynamics: several ways to slice IT

How does IT spending affect the nature of competition and the relative performance of companies within an industry? To answer those questions, we focused on three indicators—industry concentration, turbulence, and performance spread. When we aggregated data from all companies in all industries between 1965 and 2005, we noticed a consistent pattern: All indicators rose markedly in the mid-1990s for high-IT industries (those in which IT accounts for a comparatively large percentage of all fixed assets), coinciding with the surge in IT spending.

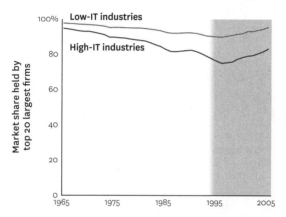

Industry Concentration: After decades of decline in all industries, industry concentration began to rise in the mid-1990s. Though the absolute level is lower, the rate of rise is faster in high-IT industries than it is in low-IT industries.

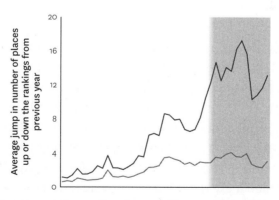

Turbulence: In turbulent markets, the top-selling company one year may not dominate the next. Today's 10th place company, for instance, might catapult

(continued)

(Continued)

to number one the following year. In less turbulent markets the same companies dominate year after year, and there's very little movement up and down in rank order. By this measure, we found consistently more sales turbulence in high-IT industries—and a marked increase in the mid-1990s.

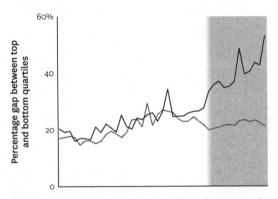

Performance Spread: The spread in gross profit margin between the company performing at the 25th percentile in its industry and the company performing at the 75th percentile—an indication of the spread between winners and losers—has grown dramatically in high-IT industries since the mid-1990s.

the mid-1990s have seen a onetime burst of innovation from IT producers, and it's simply taking IT-consuming companies a while to absorb them all. Businesses will eventually figure out how to internalize all the new tools, proponents of this theory say, and then all industries will revert to their previous competitive patterns.

While it's true that the tool kit of corporate IT has expanded a great deal in recent years, we believe that an overabundance of new technologies is not the fundamental driver of the change in dynamics we've

Is IT the Only Factor That Matters?

PREVIOUS RESEARCH SUGGESTS THAT THE changes we've observed in the competitive environment are not primarily driven by shifts in M&A activity, globalization, or R&D spending. New York University's Lawrence White, in a paper published in the *Journal of Economic Perspectives* in 2002, contended that M&A activity explained neither the decline in concentration in the first half of the 1990s nor its rise in the second half. In a 2006 research paper published in *Industrial and Corporate Change,* Harvard Business School's Pankaj Ghemawat and his colleagues found that industry concentration tends to decrease as globalization rises, implying that concentration has increased since the mid-1990s not because of more global competition but despite it.

On the other hand, Harvard professor Diego Comin and his colleagues, in their 2005 working paper "The Rise in Firm-Level Volatility," did find a correlation between companies' spending on R&D and changes in industry turbulence. So we reexamined our findings, including R&D spending in our assessments, and found that it does not detract from the significance of our IT measures. In fact, IT appears to be much more strongly correlated with the changes in competitive dynamics than R&D does.

documented. Instead, our field research suggests that businesses entered a new era of increased competitiveness in the mid-1990s not because they had so many IT innovations to choose from but because some of these new technologies enabled improvements to companies' operating models and then made it possible to replicate those improvements much more widely.

CVS offers a great example. There's no shortage of people looking to fill prescriptions—or of outlets ready to handle those orders. So CVS works hard to maintain a high level of customer service. Imagine senior management's concern, then, when surveys conducted in 2002 revealed that customer satisfaction was declining. Further analysis uncovered a key problem: Some 17% of the prescription orders were being delayed during the insurance check, which was often performed after customers had already left the store. The team decided to move the insurance check forward in the prescription fulfillment process, before the drug safety review, so all customers would still be around to answer common questions such as, "Have you changed jobs?"

This two-step process change was embedded in the information systems that supported pharmacy operations, thereby ensuring 100% compliance. The transaction screen for the drug safety review now appeared on pharmacists' computers only after all the fields in the insurance-check screen had been completed; it was simply no longer possible to do the safety review first. The redesigned protocol helped boost customer satisfaction scores without compromising safety—and not just in one store but in all of them. CVS used its enterprise information technology to replicate the new process throughout its 4,000-plus retail pharmacies nationwide within a year. Performance increased sharply, and overall customer satisfaction scores rose from 86% to 91%—a dramatic difference within the aggressive pharmacy market.

The enterprise IT underlying this initiative served two key roles. It helped the process changes stick: Clerks and pharmacists couldn't fall back on their old habits once the new protocol was embedded in the company's information systems. More important, it also allowed for quick and easy propagation of the new process to all 4,000 sites—radically amplifying the economic value of the initial innovation. Without enterprise IT, CVS could still have tried to implement this process innovation, but it would have been much more cumbersome. Updated procedure manuals might have been sent to all CVS locations, or managers may have been rotated in for training sessions and then periodically surveyed to monitor compliance. But propagating the new process digitally accelerated and magnified its competitive impact by vastly increasing the consistency of its execution throughout the organization.

Although modern commercial enterprise systems are relatively recent—SAP's ERP platform, for example, was introduced in 1992—by now, companies in virtually every industry have adopted them. According to one estimate, spending on these complex platforms already accounted for 75% of all U.S. corporate IT investment in 2001. More recently, IT consultancy Gartner Group projected that worldwide enterprise software revenue would approach $190 billion in 2008.

To understand how this profusion of enterprise IT is changing the broader competitive landscape, imagine that a drugstore chain like CVS has a number of rivals, most of which also have multiple stores. Before the advent of enterprise IT, a successful innovation by a manager at one store could lead to dominance in that manager's local market. But because no firm had a monopoly on good managers, other firms might win the competitive battle in other local markets, reflecting the relative talent at these other locations. Sharing and replication of innovations (via analog technologies like corporate memos, procedures manuals, and training sessions) would be relatively slow and imperfect, and overall market share would change little from year to year.

With the advent of enterprise IT, however, not just CVS, but its competitors have the option to deploy technology to improve their processes. Some may not exercise this option because they don't believe in the power of IT. Others will try and fail. Some will succeed, and effective innovations will spread rapidly. The firm with the best processes will win in most or all markets. At the same time, competitors will be able to strike back much more quickly: Instead of simply copying the first mover, they will introduce further IT-based innovations, perhaps instituting digitally mediated outsourcing or CRM software that identifies cross- and up-selling opportunities. These innovations will also propagate widely, rapidly, and accurately because they are embedded in the IT system. Success will prompt these companies to make bolder and more frequent competitive moves, and customers will switch from one company to another in response to them.

As a result, performance spread will rise, as the most successful IT exploiters pull away from the pack. Concentration will increase, as the losers fall by the wayside. And yet turbulence will actually intensify, as the remaining rivals use successive IT-enabled operating-model changes to leapfrog one another over time. Thus, despite the shakeout, rivalry in the industry will continue to become more fast-paced, intense, and dynamic than it was prior to the advent of enterprise technology. These are exactly the changes we see reflected in the data.

In this Schumpeterian environment, the value of process innovations greatly multiplies. This puts the onus on managers to be strategic about innovating and then propagating new ways of working.

Competing on Digital Processes

To survive, or better yet thrive, in this more competitive environment, the mantra for any CEO should be, "Deploy, innovate, and propagate": First, deploy a consistent technology platform. Then separate yourself from the pack by coming up with better ways of working. Finally, use the platform to propagate these business innovations widely and reliably. In this regard, deploying IT serves two distinct roles—as a catalyst for innovative ideas and as an engine for delivering them. Each of the three steps in the mantra presents different and critical management challenges, not least of which have to do with questions of centralization and autonomy.

Deployment: the management challenge

Since the mid-1990s, the commercial availability of enterprise software packages has added a new item to the list of senior management's responsibilities: Determining which aspects of their companies' operating models should be globally (or at least widely) consistent, then using technology to replicate them with high

The Elements of a Successful IT-Enabled Process

GIVEN THE COSTS OF ENTERPRISE IT and the risks inherent in deploying it poorly, it's especially important that the change projects you select capitalize on IT's strengths. Consider the following hypothetical example of a company that did just that.

A U.S. furniture maker sells both standard and custom pieces out of its 100 showrooms nationwide. Because salespeople in each of the showrooms have very little direct interaction with or information about the company's three factories, they all quote long lead times for custom furniture, just to be on the safe side.

To rectify this situation, the company develops software to integrate the activities of manufacturing and sales, and tests it at one location. Now salespeople can enter the specifications of a custom order and instantly receive an accurate delivery date.

The company also decides to use the software to manage customer deliveries. The delivery team for the test showroom is required to call back to the dispatch center immediately after leaving a customer's house. That enables the center to contact the customer to verify his or her satisfaction and address any concerns. The software tracks delivery times and satisfaction levels and finds the former is decreasing while the latter ticks upward.

Recognizing its success, the company quickly embeds the new process in its enterprise software and rolls it out to the other 99 locations. Because customers value these process innovations, the company's market share grows nationwide.

---

fidelity. Some top teams have pounced on the opportunity. Many more, however, have embraced this responsibility only reluctantly, unwilling to tackle two formidable barriers to deployment: *fragmentation* and *autonomy*.

Successful IT-enabled business process improvements like this one generally have a number of important characteristics:

They cover a wide span. The new ways of working apply across a very large swath of a company—in this case, all stores, factories, and delivery teams.

They produce results immediately. As soon as the new enterprise system goes live, so do the process changes it enables.

They are precise, rather than general guidelines, suggesting highly scripted instructions for business activities (furniture order taking and delivery).

They are consistent—executed the same way everywhere, every time. Every furniture store uses the same method to quote lead times, and deliveries are closed out the same way day after day.

They make monitoring easy. Activities and events can be observed and tracked in real time, providing unprecedented opportunities for testing and feedback.

They build in enforceability. The designers of a new process that's embedded in IT can have great confidence that it will be executed as intended. It is often simply impossible to execute the process the old way, and even when backsliding is possible it can be recognized and addressed. The furniture company could easily use the data collected during the delivery process to determine if all teams were calling in properly.

Historically, regional, product, and function managers have been given a great deal of leeway to purchase, install, and customize IT systems as they see fit. But bitter experience has shown that it's prohibitively time-consuming and expensive to stitch together a jumble of legacy systems so they can all use common data, and support and enforce standardized processes. Even if a company invests heavily in standardized enterprise software for the entire organization, it may not remain standard for long, as the software is deployed in ways other than it was originally intended in dozens, or even hundreds, of separate instances. When that happens, it's almost certain that data, processes, customer interfaces, and operating models will become inconsistent—thus defeating the whole competitive purpose of purchasing the package in the first place.

That's what initially happened at networking giant Cisco. In the mid-1990s, Cisco successfully implemented a single ERP platform throughout the company. Managers were then given the green light to purchase and install as many applications as they wanted, to sit on that platform. Cisco's IT department helped the various functions, technology groups, and product lines throughout the world get their desired programs up and running without attempting to constrain or second-guess their decisions.

When newly arrived CIO Brad Boston assessed Cisco's IT environment in 2001, he found that system, data, and process fragmentation was an unintended consequence of the company's enthusiasm for technology. There were, for example, nine different tools for checking the status of a customer order. Each pulled information from different repositories and defined key terms in different ways. The multiple databases and fuzzy terms resulted in the circulation of conflicting order-status reports around the company. Boston's assessment also revealed that there were over 50 different customer-survey tools, 15 different business-intelligence applications, and more than 200 additional IT projects in progress.

Deployment efforts heighten the tensions—present in every sizable company—between global consistency and local autonomy. As the Cisco example shows, however, this conflict often exists by default rather than by design. Ultimately, the top team's focused efforts to manage this tension reaped tremendous benefits.

Responding to the CIO's assessment, senior managers decided to upgrade Cisco's original ERP system and other key applications to support standardized data and processes. The upgrade was budgeted at $200 million over three years. Cisco identified several key business processes—market to sell, lead to order, quote to cash, issue to resolution, forecast to build, idea to product, and hire to retire—and configured its systems to support the subprocesses involved in each stage. The software updates and the strategy discussions the technology engendered eventually resulted in greater consistency throughout the organization and contributed to Cisco's strong performance over the past few years.

At about the same time that Cisco was untangling its legacy spaghetti, the leader of a much older and more traditional company was also reimagining the kinds of information systems his firm would need to compete more successfully. When Ari Bousbib became president of Otis in 2002, the information systems of the 149-year-old company were not so much fragmented as virtually nonexistent. As Harvard Business School's F. Warren

McFarlan and Brian J. DeLacey recounted in a 2005 case study, the software applications in place were largely antiquated for implementing the critical processes of gathering customer requests to install a new elevator system, specifying the exact configuration of the order, and creating a final proposal. In many regions, in fact, the processes were still being done entirely on paper.

Like Cisco, Otis took a hard look at its core processes and ended up replacing old software with a new enterprise technology platform the company called e*Logistics. It was designed to connect sales, factory, and field operations worldwide through the internet. Otis defined four processes—sales, order fulfillment, field installation, and job closing—and designed e*Logistics to ensure that improvements in the way each process was carried out occurred uniformly, every time, everywhere. Eventually, Otis realized not only significantly shorter sales-cycle times but higher revenues and operating profit.

Innovation: IT-enabled opportunities

Data analytics drawn from enterprise IT applications, along with collective intelligence and other Web 2.0 technologies, can be important aides not just in propagating ideas but also in generating them. They are certainly no replacement for brilliant insights from a line manager or a eureka moment during a meeting, but they can complement and speed the search for business process innovations.

UK grocery chain Tesco is one company that employs enterprise IT's aggregation and analysis capabilities in this way. Like many retailers around the world, it uses customer-rewards cards to collect detailed data about individuals' purchases, to categorize customers, and to tailor offers accordingly. But the grocer goes a step further, tracking redemption rates in great detail and performing experiments to tweak its processes to get a better response from customers. In an industry where the average redemption rate for direct-marketing initiatives is about 2%, Babson professor Tom Davenport has noted, Tesco's data analytics help drive its rate to approximately 20%.

Web 2.0 applications that bring collective wisdom to the fore can also uncover potential business innovations. Jim Lavoie, CEO of the technology firm Rite-Solutions, built something called a "Mutual Fun" market within the company's intranet that has three indices employees can invest in—Savings Bonds for ideas on saving costs, Bow Jones for ideas on extending existing products, and Spazdaq for new product concepts. Any Rite-Solutions employee can suggest a new idea in any of these markets. Workers can also view the "prospectus of ideas," invest play money in them, and even sign up to complete any tasks necessary to make those concepts reality. As Lavoie said in a recent online interview with the nonprofit Business Innovation Factory: "We believe the next brilliant idea is going to come from somebody other than senior management, and unless you're trying to harvest those ideas, you're not going to get them....That's why we give everybody an equal voice, and a game to provoke their intellectual curiosity."

Propagation: top down and bottom up

Part of the attraction of enterprise systems has been the opportunity for management to impose best practices and standardized procedures universally, as CVS did to great advantage, and so eliminate the chaos of inconsistent homegrown practices. There's really no competitive advantage in having each department develop and use its own idiosyncratic process for inventory control, for instance, especially when best practices already exist.

While an ERP system is an obvious tool for propagation, other technologies are also important, and they show that innovations do not necessarily emanate from headquarters. For instance, Web 2.0 applications can help process changes emerge organically from lower levels in an organization. Within Cisco, for instance, a community of about 10,000 Macintosh users was dissatisfied with the level of support they were receiving from the company's central IT group. But instead of complaining, they created a wiki to share ideas about how to use their Macs more effectively. They posted information, files, links, and applications that could be edited by any user—tips and tricks that ultimately became huge productivity enhancers. In this case, process innovations flowed through the company to its great benefit without central management direction.

The role of decision rights.

At first glance, the Cisco and Otis examples seem to support the view that propagating processes using enterprise IT necessarily leads to more centralized companies—ones in which most of the important decisions are made at the top and the rest of the business exists only to execute them. Many of the choices about core business processes and the systems that support them were taken out of the hands of business-unit leaders and regional managers, and the companies' change efforts appeared to lead to higher levels of centralization than had previously existed. But the reality is more complicated.

Even as some decisions become centralized and standardized, others are pushed outward from headquarters. Senior executives do play a primary role in identifying and propagating critical business processes, but line managers and employees often end up with more discretion within these processes to serve customer needs and to apply tacit, idiosyncratic, or relationship-specific information that only they have. To appreciate how important this distinction is, consider an analogy from government. The process of writing a constitution is inherently a highly centralized activity—a small group of framers makes decisions on behalf of an entire population. It's perfectly possible, and in fact common, however, for that constitution to define a highly decentralized government.

At both Cisco and Otis, local managers and frontline employees retained critical responsibilities in their companies' IT-enabled operating models—and often gained new ones. After e*Logistics was put in place at Otis, for example, field installation supervisors became responsible for the first time for certifying that a site was ready to install an elevator before it would be shipped. (In the old operating model, the equipment was simply shipped as soon as it was manufactured.) The new business practice was standardized throughout the world, but it was not centralized. It actually placed more responsibility in the hands of frontline employees.

Consider, too, the Spanish clothing company Zara. It has more than 1,000 stores worldwide, and they all order clothes exactly the same way, using the same digital form, following a rigid weekly timetable for placing orders. Most other large apparel retailers rely on sophisticated forecasting algorithms, executed by computers at headquarters, to determine which clothes will sell in each location and in what quantities. Headquarters pushes these clothes down to stores with virtually no input from their managers. Zara's store managers, however, have almost complete discretion over which clothes to order; they choose them based on local tastes and immediate demand.

This sharp difference between Zara's and other retailers' approaches to the same challenge highlights a critically important point: We don't expect that enterprise IT will inevitably lead to one best way to execute core processes. In fact, it can prompt a great deal of experimentation and variation, as companies try to understand who has the most relevant knowledge to make decisions and where, ultimately, to site decision rights.

Maximizing Return on Talent

As corporate IT facilitates the implementation and monitoring of processes, the value of simply carrying out rote instructions will fall while the value of inventing better methods will rise. In some cases, this may even lead to a "superstar" effect, as disproportionate rewards accrue to the very best knowledge workers. Human resource policies and corporate culture will need to evolve to support this type of worker. An effective leader and a well-designed organization will need not only to aggressively seek out and identify such individuals and the innovations they generate but also to develop and reward them appropriately.

An analysis of 400 U.S. companies that Erik Brynjolfsson published with Wharton professor Lorin Hitt in 2005, found that organizations successfully using IT were significantly more aggressive in vetting new hires: They considered more applicants. They scrutinized each one more intensively. They involved senior management (not just HR) early and often in the interview process. After identifying top talent, these firms invested substantially more time and money on both internal and external training and education. Furthermore, they gave their employees more discretion in how to do their jobs while linking their compensation and rewards—including promotions—more tightly to performance using a suite of metrics that was more detailed than competitors'. The costs of managing talent in this way may be high, but the payoff increases exponentially if you can leverage the talents of a high-performing manager at one location to maximize results in thousands of sites worldwide.

———————

The arrival of powerful new information technologies does not render obsolete all previous assumptions and insights about how to do business, but it does open up new opportunities to executives. Our research has led us to three conclusions: First of all, the data show that IT has sharpened differences among companies instead of reducing them. This reflects the fact that while companies have always varied widely in their ability to select, adopt, and exploit innovations, technology has accelerated and amplified these differences. Second, line executives matter: Highly qualified vendors, consultants, and IT departments might be necessary for the successful implementation of enterprise technologies themselves, but the real value comes from the process innovations that can now be delivered on those platforms. Fostering the right innovations and propagating them widely are both executive responsibilities—ones that can't be delegated. Finally, the competitive shakeup brought on by IT is not nearly complete, even in the IT-intensive U.S. economy. We expect to see these altered competitive dynamics in other countries, as well, as their IT investments grow.

It is not easy for most companies to deploy enterprise IT successfully. The technologies themselves are complicated to configure and test, and changing people's behavior and attitudes toward technology is even more challenging. Enterprise IT typically changes many jobs in major ways; this is never an easy sell to either employees or line managers. As the performance spread, concentration, and churn increase, management becomes a distinctly less comfortable profession—more unforgiving of mistakes, faster to weed out low performers. Even those executives who are prepared will not necessarily survive the inevitable turbulence. But those who do can expect outsize rewards—at least until another player comes along and uses IT to propagate a business innovation that's even better.

ANDREW MCAFEE is a principal research scientist at MIT's Center for Digital Business. **ERIK BRYNJOLFSSON** is the Schussel Family Professor at the MIT Sloan School of Management and the director of MIT's Center for Digital Business.

Originally published in July 2008. Reprint R0807J

Empowered

by Josh Bernoff and Ted Schadler

MAYBE YOU'VE HEARD ABOUT THE musician Dave Carroll and his experience as a United Air Lines customer. He was so incensed that the company rejected his damage claim after its baggage handlers broke his guitar that he made a catchy YouTube video, "United Breaks Guitars." Eight million people have already viewed this decidedly negative take on the United brand.

Carroll's reaction is hardly unique. The popular mommy blogger Heather Armstrong was so upset over the failure of her Maytag washer and the company's ensuing service missteps that, using her mobile phone, she told her million-plus followers on Twitter they should never buy a Maytag. Greenpeace supporters barraged Nestlé's Facebook page with complaints about how the company's sourcing policies lead to environmental damage. The list of examples is endless, because these days anyone with a smartphone or a computer can instantly inflict lasting brand damage.

But it's not just cranky customers who can use readily available, powerful, hyperconnected technologies to make an impact. Employees can, too. Mark Betka and Tim Receveur, of the U.S. State Department, used off-the-shelf software called Adobe Connect to create Co.Nx, a public diplomacy outreach project that presents webchats with U.S. government officials, businesspeople, and others. The webchats now have international audiences in the tens of thousands and more than 100,000 Facebook fans. At Black & Decker, Rob Sharpe uses homemade online video for sales training, just as Dave Carroll used it to lash out at United. Paul Vienick, in charge of product development for E*Trade, made E*Trade Mobile Pro possible—he used mobile to serve customers and build loyalty, just as Heather Armstrong used it to attack Maytag.

You can build a strategy around empowering employees to solve customers' problems—but it will challenge your organization from the inside. Freeing employees to experiment with new technologies, to make high-profile decisions on the fly, to build systems that customers see, and to effectively speak for the organization in public is not something most corporations or government agencies are accustomed to doing.

They may be concerned, for example, about how employees will use the technology. After all, part of Nestlé's problem with Facebook was the clumsy response of its own employees to the Greenpeace attack. But in this age of smartphones and broadband, employees can't be blocked from doing inappropriate things. It would not have been possible to stop the Domino's employees who posted a video on YouTube of themselves pretending to perform unsanitary acts on customers' pizzas.

Idea in Brief

After his guitar was broken on a United Air Lines flight and the airline rejected his damage claim, musician Dave Carroll made the YouTube video "United Breaks Guitars," which more than 8 million people have viewed. Carroll is far from alone in having employed social media to lambaste a company for poor customer service. For example, one popular blogger advised her million-plus followers on Twitter not to buy Maytag appliances. But the very technologies that empower customers can also empower employees, write Bernoff and Schadler, of Forrester Research. Companies can build a strategy around freeing employees to experiment with new technologies, make high-profile decisions on the fly, and effectively speak for the organization in public. Companies that feel hesitant to give their employees such freedom can benefit from what the authors call the HERO Compact—whereby management, IT, and HEROes (for "highly empowered and resourceful operatives") agree to work together to manage technological innovations. Management contracts to encourage innovation and manage risk, IT to support and scale employees' projects, and HEROes to innovate within a safe framework. Best Buy, Black & Decker, Vail Resorts, and Aflac are among the companies that have empowered their employees to take full advantage of social media. But it takes a while for corporate cultures to embrace this sort of innovation. In the meantime, managers can move forward on their own—building internal communities, looking outside the company for creative strategies, reviewing their hiring practices, and reaching out to customer-facing departments.

Far better than trying to prevent such activity is to acknowledge that your employees have technology power. Then you can set policy, train them in permissible communications and activities, and harness their creativity as a strategic force to power your company. Armed with technology, your employees can build solutions at the speed of today's connected customers.

They're ready to do so. But if you're like most managers, your company isn't yet set up to make this activity possible. It could be. It could behave like Best Buy.

Best Buy Empowers Its Staff

Best Buy is just as susceptible to online customer complaints as any other company, but because it's run differently, it can respond differently. A good example is Twelpforce. More than 2,500 Best Buy employees have signed up for this system, which enables them to see Best Buy–related problems that customers have aired on Twitter and respond to them. Twelpforce includes customer service staff, in-store sales associates (called Blue Shirts), and Geek Squad, the service reps who make house calls for technical assistance.

Here's an example of how Twelpforce works: Earlier this year Josh Korin bought an iPhone, along with an insurance plan, from Best Buy in Chicago. When the iPhone stopped working, the in-store staff offered him a BlackBerry as a loaner replacement. That wasn't what he felt he deserved after buying the insurance plan, so he began tweeting about his disappointment. Even though it was over a weekend, a customer service rep, Coral Biegler, responded quickly on Twitter. By the next day she had arranged for him to get a replacement iPhone. Korin changed his tune and began tweeting about how great Best Buy's service was. So did his wife, who has more than 3,000 Twitter followers.

Twelpforce exists because Best Buy empowers its employees to come up with technological solutions.

Gary Koelling, a social media expert in Best Buy's marketing group, helped originate the idea. Ben Hedrington, a technology staffer in the e-commerce group, figured out in a week of evenings how to tap Google's cloud computing service to build a Twitter system serving multiple employees. John Bernier, a marketing manager, took charge of the project and triumphed over legal obstacles, including labor laws.

Best Buy's leaders support technological innovation regardless of where in the organization it comes from. Barry Judge, the company's CMO, has made it a priority to identify and encourage new ideas like Twelpforce. "We're almost always in a half-baked mode" when it comes to ideas, Judge says. "Half-baked ideas allow people [both internally and externally] to give you feedback." Judge's marketing department is always learning. "If you are not curious, you won't last long in marketing," he says. "You have to have some failures to see that."

The results of this attitude are visible throughout Best Buy's marketing. For example, Judge posts the company's TV commercials on his blog before they start airing. In one case, commenters from outside the company complained about a lack of sensitivity in a commercial describing how a Blue Shirt helped a customer in the armed forces. The commercial never aired. Best Buy has also taken the innovative step of opening up the programming interfaces to BestBuy.com, allowing other websites to alert people of price changes, for example. All these activities were developed by marketing staffers. All involved risk. And all went forward.

The HERO Compact

Because of the image it evokes, we use the term HERO ("highly empowered and resourceful operative") for people who innovate with technology inside a company. HEROes exist because technologies like Twitter, online communities, cloud computing, and online video are so easy to master and so cheap to set up. Employees, especially in marketing, sales, and customer service, see customers' problems and use these technologies to solve them. Moving forward with their solutions creates challenges for three groups: the HEROes themselves, management, and IT.

Most companies aren't set up to harness technological innovation that comes from outside IT. Their IT departments can't launch and run these sorts of projects—they're too far from customers and typically lack the budget and staff. Even so, they're uncomfortable (often with good reason) when marketers and others move forward with technology. As for managers, both senior and midlevel, they want to encourage innovation but worry about the risks associated with these projects. And the HEROes have trouble executing their plans at scale in the absence of consistent support.

In most companies, cultural resistance to empowering employees to use technology is systemwide. Keeping technology locked down and under the IT department's control seems like the safe thing to do. It limits risk and prevents chaos. This traditional approach would be fine if not for the actions of all those empowered customers. Companies have to respond to customers' escalating

The HERO Compact: who does what

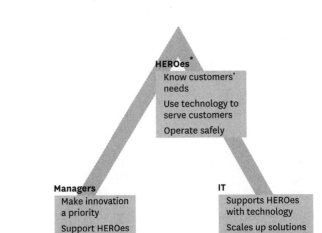

HEROes *
- Know customers' needs
- Use technology to serve customers
- Operate safely

Managers
- Make innovation a priority
- Support HEROes
- Work with IT to manage risk

IT
- Supports HEROes with technology
- Scales up solutions
- Provides tools to manage risk

*"Highly empowered and resourceful operatives"

power. Their employees are ready to do so. The challenge is to encourage HERO-driven innovation without generating chaos.

A crucial part of the solution is what we call the HERO Compact—an agreement among the three groups to work together to manage technological innovation. Under the compact:

HEROes agree to innovate within a safe framework. The employees who come up with these projects must work within business structures. They must respond to support from management and IT by innovating in directions that align with corporate strategy and by observing security, legal, and other corporate policies. Having succeeded with a project, a HERO is responsible for spreading newly won knowledge to others in the organization who might benefit from it.

Managers agree to encourage innovation and manage risk. Managers must communicate their openness to employee innovation, not just with words but by recognizing examples publicly and not punishing failures. To ensure that HERO activity is productive, managers must also clearly and regularly communicate strategic goals. And they must work with IT to understand and deal with the risks associated with HERO projects, modifying them or even shutting them down if the legal or regulatory risks are out of line with any expected benefit.

IT agrees to support and scale up HERO projects. IT needs to advise HEROes and keep them safe. At PTC, a Massachusetts-based supplier of computer-aided design and product life-cycle management software, after the marketing department came up with the idea for a customer community and provided funding, IT played a key role in evaluating technology vendors for the community. IT must assess and mitigate risk and then give managers the tools to understand the risks in the context of the business benefits. It must also recognize when HERO projects have become strategic and help scale them up.

None of this can succeed unless the company and its technology policies are ready. (See the sidebar "Is Your

Company Ready for Empowered Employees?") But when it does work, HERO-driven, incremental innovation wells up from every customer-facing department. This radically improves the agility with which companies can address the needs of their empowered customers. Let's look at some more examples.

Video Training at Black & Decker

Rob Sharpe is the director of sales training at Black & Decker (now part of Stanley Black & Decker). The company's hundreds of sales staffers must explain and sell a multitude of complex products to retailers as huge as Home Depot and as small as mom-and-pop hardware stores. The market is highly competitive. Although the company had been doing effective sales training using PowerPoint and an in-house learning system, Sharpe conceived of a new approach after taking a look at YouTube.

As a pilot project, Sharpe gave out $150, simple-to-use Flip video cameras and free video editing software to several dozen salespeople in the training program. His reasoning: "I'm a visual learner; a lot of these tool guys are visual learners." One of his trainees, back out in the field, sent in a video that showed the weaknesses of a competitor's product. Both the training staff and other salespeople immediately "got it," seeing how effective video could be for Black & Decker sales.

More video started pouring in. Salespeople began documenting challenges, product features, and effective sales solutions. Video cameras became a standard part of

Is Your Company Ready for Empowered Employees?

IN LATE 2009 WE SURVEYED more than 5,000 information workers about their use of and attitudes toward "do-it-yourself" technology—that is, applications and websites not sanctioned by their companies. We identified two dimensions that determine whether people are able and willing to innovate in creating customer solutions.

The first dimension is cultural. We asked the workers if they agreed with the statement "I feel empowered to solve my own problems and challenges at work." Because people tend to respond positively to this statement, we counted someone as feeling empowered only if his or her response was eight or higher on a 10-point scale.

All information workers

Only 20% of the workers both feel empowered and act resourceful. The key employees whom we call HEROes ("highly empowered and resourceful operatives") come from that upper-right quadrant.

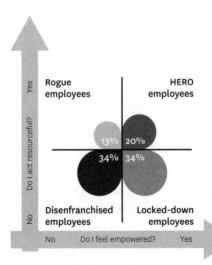

The second dimension is practical. We asked the workers if they had downloaded and regularly used at least two applications not authorized by their employers (such as a video editing application and a web browser) or if they regularly visited at least two websites that require a login but weren't authorized (such as LinkedIn and an online project collaboration site). We counted people who engaged in either of these activities as acting resourceful.

Technology products and services workers

Further analysis reveals patterns by industry. The technology products and services industry, with 37% of its workers in the HERO quadrant, is far more likely than other industries to generate employee-created innovations. (The industries with the lowest proportion of information workers in the HERO quadrant are retail, government, health care, and education.)

Rogue employees

HERO employees

17% 37%

19% 27%

Disenfranchised employees

Locked-down employees

Marketing and sales staff

We also analyzed workers by job description. Among those in marketing and sales (excluding retail sales workers), 35% are HEROes, meaning that they have great potential for creative innovation—a fact we saw reflected in the many new technology and social applications coming out of marketing departments in the companies we researched.

Rogue employees

HERO employees

20% 35%

22% 23%

Disenfranchised employees

Locked-down employees

sales training. According to Sharpe, "Now we get 15 to 20 videos a month—how power tools are used on job sites, feedback on the tools. And the content is already completely edited," ready for viewing.

"I will not let people in this department create a 45-minute course again," Sharpe says. "It's not what the staff need or what they want. Speed to execution is just as important. The training staff can spend a half hour with the product, come up with our own opinions and competitive analysis, and send [a video] out the next day with an assessment."

The most popular videos are viewed by more than half of Black & Decker's sales force. Training that used to take two weeks now takes one. New staff members spend 15 hours online before even coming to the training center. Senior management, corporate marketing, and public relations people review the collection for useful bits of content and motivational nuggets.

Black & Decker's IT department was reluctant at first, citing concerns about security and space on the server. Now it's an enthusiastic supporter. And Sharpe's manager, Les Ireland, then Black & Decker's president of commercial operations in North America, supported his efforts.

"The concept of getting our teams involved in delivering 'real world' content was a powerful idea," Ireland says. He also likes the increase in speed and agility: "How quickly we can execute a new technology in order to capture the productivity across our commercial team is always a critical question." Black & Decker's success with video illustrates a broader point:

Regardless of where the HERO projects we've studied began, they grew fastest when management and IT were on board.

Social Media Marketing at Vail Resorts

Vail Resorts operates multiple properties, including five major ski resorts. The company found that its traditional advertising strategy—space in *Ski* magazine and other long-lead publications—was becoming ineffective; customers had begun booking ski vacations only weeks or days in advance. Vail needed to create pitches tailored to what was happening at the moment—snowfall, competitors' promotions, local events.

Vail's CEO, Rob Katz, decided to remake his marketing plan, with a focus on short-lead media such as newspapers and internet sites. He also decided to embrace Facebook and Twitter, where many skiers now get their information. "We needed to be a leader in [the social] space, rather than battle the trend of where our customers are going," he says.

Katz hired Mike Slone, an interactive development veteran, to head up social engagement in the new marketing strategy. Slone manages five staffers at Vail's corporate headquarters who respond to tweets, blogs, and other social-media inquiries. He also works to involve other staff members, including the heads of online marketing at each of the company's five mountain resorts. One of their tasks is creating videos of activity on the slopes and posting them as soon as possible. In essence, Vail uses customers themselves to generate a sense of fun, exciting and helping to recruit other customers.

Katz sends signals from the top showing the level of creativity and responsiveness to customers that he'd like to see. He himself tweets, as @rickysridge. When a customer named Bob Lefsetz tweeted about a problem he'd had signing up for a meal pass, Katz responded and made sure that one of his staffers got Lefsetz what he was looking for. It turned out that Lefsetz is an acerbic and popular blogger in the music industry who has nearly 13,000 Twitter followers. After this exchange they read about how great Vail is rather than getting a "United Breaks Guitars"-style rant.

Katz and the other HERO-friendly managers we've surveyed have a common attitude toward their staffs and employee innovation. First, they clearly communicate corporate priorities (such as the shift to short-lead media). Second, they encourage experimentation— within the bounds of maintaining brand image and avoiding identifiable security risks. Third, they tolerate failure as long as it leads to learning. And fourth, they create systems and structures within their companies that bust silos, which enables HEROes to share their learning and connect with others facing similar challenges.

IT Prodding and Support at Aflac

Gerald Shields, the chief information officer of the supplemental insurance provider Aflac, has plenty to do. He manages 600 IT professionals and a $135 million budget. His people operate the systems that keep Aflac's transactions flowing and the networks that bind the company together. But he finds time to prod the rest of the company into coming up with technology projects for customer service.

Shields educated his direct reports and Paul Amos, Aflac's president, about social technologies. Then he went to work on Jeff Charney, the chief marketing officer. The combination of management support and IT backing proved powerful. Amos and Charney convened managers from all over the company for a workshop on social-technology opportunities. Several cross-functional groups left the workshop charged with creating actionable plans for social applications. Shields and Charney then selected the two most promising ideas that emerged: an online community for Aflac's 80,000 independent sales associates, and one for 200,000 billing and payroll administrators at customer companies.

The independent sales associates' community is called The Buzz. Aflac's field salespeople close thousands of deals a month; when they can connect with one another and with their service and marketing support teams, they learn rapidly. Each month 2,800 sales associates visit The Buzz.

Duck Pond is the community that serves billing and payroll administrators. These people didn't make the decision to buy Aflac, but they're a key group in getting its benefits delivered effectively. They also value connecting to people in similar jobs, because they typically work in human resources or finance, with few internal peers. Duck Pond was created not only to share information about Aflac but also to help the administrators get support from the company and from their peers on all sorts of issues, not just those related to insurance. As Shields puts it, "We don't want you to think of Aflac as just a supplemental insurance company. We want you to say, 'Wait a minute—I'm on Duck Pond all the time.'"

Too often we've seen companies launch social applications without IT support and hit a scaling or integration or security wall. Gerald Shields stands out for stimulating innovation from product, marketing, and sales support groups even though he won't own the results. His initiative got management on board, and management benefited as the innovation spread throughout the company. And Shields can steer HERO activity in what he believes will be productive technological directions.

HERO-Driven Innovation for B2B

The dynamics that lead to HERO-driven innovation depend on customers' and employees' using powerful, readily accessible technology. They don't depend on the industry those customers are in or on whether a company sells to businesses or consumers.

It's a commonly held fallacy that consumers use social applications more than businesses do. But our surveys of business buyers show that 95% use social technologies and 76% use them for work—a higher level of participation than among consumers. Mobile technologies in particular are important, as demonstrated by the ubiquity of smartphones for business communication.

PTC, the software supplier, went forward with an online social community because surveys of its business customers showed overwhelming support for such outreach. Black & Decker's sales staff sells to buyers at retail chains, and Aflac's customers are businesses as well. HEROes can innovate, IT can support their innovation, and managers can reap the rewards regardless of whether a company sells to consumers or to businesses.

Building a HERO-Powered Business

Companies that want to encourage this sort of innovation should embrace the HERO Compact. But even when they do, it takes a while for corporate cultures to change. In the meantime, managers throughout the organization can move forward on their own, stimulating and rewarding HERO activity.

If you are a manager or other employee who has come up with a solution—that is, if you're a potential HERO—the first step is to evaluate your idea: How many different departments will need a say? How difficult to deploy is the technology? How big a budget will you need? Then look not only at the value you will create, but also at how you can *prove* that value, in decreased costs, increased revenues, additional leads, or other metrics that matter to the business. Unless you've assessed both the effort and the value, you can't really know whether your project is worth doing—or whether you'll be able to convince management that it's worth doing.

We also recommend looking for similar projects in the enterprise. Look for people who are using the same technologies you're using (say, online communities and Twitter), but also for people facing the same challenges (such as working with PR and customer service). You'll learn a lot from those who have trodden the same ground and faced the same obstacles. Build an internal community to find and collaborate with these people.

For higher-level managers, the key is not just encouragement but visibility. Simply urging people to be more creative doesn't work. Instead, identify the kinds of solutions you're looking for—outside as well as inside your company. At General Mills, for example, marketing leaders hold monthly department meetings where they highlight creative strategies used by other brands and industries.

You might also want to review your hiring practices. Find people who are conversant with online social networks, online video, web services, and social applications. Their skills will help raise the level of innovation in your department.

If you're in IT, you don't have to be the CIO to behave like Gerald Shields. Reach out to marketing, sales, and other customer-facing departments—and go out to meet customers. IT's reputation for standoffishness can dissolve after a few face-to-face meetings. Concentrate a little more on saying "Yes, and here's how," and less on saying "No, that's unsafe/too expensive/not possible." The payoff is in becoming more plugged in, more relevant, and more valuable.

What Is Your Company's Future?

With all this powerful, inexpensive, easily accessible technology available, every manager has a choice. You can fight your employees' natural impulse to connect with customers and build solutions. You can lock down the systems, ask IT to block the sites, and ensure that no unauthorized technology-driven activity takes place. Given smartphones, countless free web services, and people who own their own laptops, you're unlikely to succeed. But you will spend a lot of energy proving to your employees that you don't trust them and you don't want them to innovate. And you'll be defenseless when the next Dave Carroll or Heather Armstrong comes after your brand.

Or you can recognize that your employees are the solution to customers' problems and find ways to stimulate, harness, and channel their innovations. You can acknowledge their activity and manage the risks to keep them and your company safe as well as responsive.

Our research shows that technological innovation can now come from anywhere in a company. What makes the difference is whether the company has organized itself so that its creative people can become HEROes.

JOSH BERNOFF is the senior vice president for idea development at Forrester Research and a coauthor of *Groundswell: Winning in a World Transformed by Social Technologies* (Harvard Business Review Press, 2008). **TED SCHADLER** is a principal analyst at Forrester Research. Portions of this article were adapted from *Empowered* (Harvard Business Review Press, 2010).

Originally published in July 2010. Reprint R1007H

Index